A MAN'S GUIDE TO
LIVING AUTHENTICALLY,
OVERCOMING ADVERSITY,
AND RECLAIMING MASCULINITY

FORGED IN BRAVERY

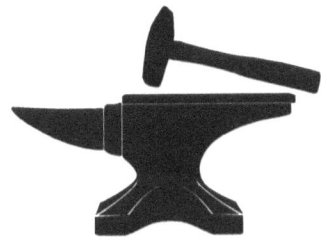

JOHN ROBERT HATFIELD

This book is intended as a reference volume only. It is sold with the understanding that the publisher and author are not engaged in rendering any professional services. The information given here is designed to help you make informed decisions. If you suspect that you have a problem that might require professional treatment or advice, you should seek competent help.

The stories and factual accounts in this book have been fictionalized and altered to protect the privacy of the individuals and their families. Persons referenced in this book may be composites or entirely fictitious, thus references to any real persons, living or dead, is not implied.

Published by River Grove Books
Austin, TX
www.rivergrovebooks.com

Copyright ©2023 John Robert Hatfield

All rights reserved.

Thank you for purchasing an authorized edition of this book and for complying with copyright law. No part of this book may be reproduced, stored in a retrieval system, or transmitted by any means, electronic, mechanical, photocopying, recording, or otherwise, without written permission from the copyright holder.

Distributed by River Grove Books

Design and composition by Greenleaf Book Group
Cover design by Greenleaf Book Group
Cover images used under license from
©Shutterstock.com/HolyCrazyLazy; ©Shutterstock.com/Aphelleon;
©Shutterstock.com/Atlnts99

Publisher's Cataloging-in-Publication data is available.

Print ISBN: 978-1-63299-754-8

eBook ISBN: 978-1-63299-755-5

First Edition

In memory of
John and Doris Hatfield

Indelible are the words
I love you
I'm proud of you.

Indelible are the values
Sacrifice,
Responsibility,
and
Family.

Indelible is the action
Always choosing to initiate regardless of my rejection.

To all the older men
To all the men my age
To all the younger men
Who made me into the man I am today,
To you I give honor
To you I say thanks.

"I am a person through other people."
—Zulu proverb called Ubuntu

To Dr. Kristin Kahler
Without you I wouldn't be where I'm at today
Always Grateful

> "Show me the man you honor, and I will know what kind of man you are, for it shows me what your ideal of manhood is and what kind of man you long to be."
>
> —THOMAS CARLYLE

CONTENTS

INTRODUCTION 1

PART 1: STEP INTO THE ARENA

CHAPTER 1: The Fork in the Road 9

CHAPTER 2: The Relational Fear Arena 27

CHAPTER 3: The Professional Fear Arena 43

CHAPTER 4: The Private Fear Arena 63

CHAPTER 5: Taking Your Licks. 69

CHAPTER 6: Anger Issues. 95

PART 2: WHAT DOES IT MEAN TO BE A MAN?

CHAPTER 7: Fake Masculinity 107

CHAPTER 8: True Masculinity 121

CHAPTER 9: Using Your Masculine Power for Good . . . 147

CHAPTER 10: The Importance of Male Friendships 155

CHAPTER 11: Are You Strong Enough to Be Vulnerable? . 171

CHAPTER 12: Braveass Virtues 181

NOTES 211

ABOUT THE AUTHOR. 217

INTRODUCTION

FOR MORE THAN TWENTY-FIVE YEARS, I HAVE BEEN INVOLVED WITH men in university, business, and family settings. My life calling is to develop and empower men. My greatest attributes are my brokenness and my mistakes. Over the years, I have been involved with hundreds of men who have achieved personal and professional success, yet they found themselves wounded, lonely, longing for male friendships, confused concerning masculinity and yet desiring their masculinity to matter, afraid, and struggling to navigate adversity. I suspect some of these same issues they've shared with me and many I have gone through myself may be familiar to you.

We seem to be confused about which virtues represent us as men and our need to be committed to embracing and developing them in our lives. We often think we need to be a badass, full of aggression and threatening violence. But it's much harder and more rewarding to be *braveass*. Braveass virtues include sacrifice, responsibility, hard work, owning our mistakes, integrity, self-control, self-discipline, honesty, humility, vulnerability, and learning to lead ourselves. Mostly, we don't think about it too much and are surprised when we learn what we think makes a man. When asked what traits society values most in boys, "only 2 percent of male survey respondents said *honesty* and *morality*," says Peggy Orenstein in her article, "The Miseducation of the American Boy."[1]

I frequently ask fraternity audiences the following series of questions: Who is more masculine, the football player or the guy in the marching band? The answer to this first question is always resounding: the football player. I then ask why they demoted the guy in the marching band to second class in his masculinity. Next, I ask which man is more masculine, the wrestler or the golfer. True to form, the answer is the wrestler. Once again, I ask why the golfer didn't get the man card. Finally, I ask whether a soldier, the guy on the football team, or the wrestler is the most masculine. Yup, you guessed it, the soldier gets the masculine distinction medal. Once again, I ask them why he got the top award and what that says about the other two.

As I look into the audience, their faces look dumbfounded, and it suddenly gets quiet. It's like I take a two-by-four and hit them between the eyes; they're dazed. Obviously, they have never been challenged with how they define their male identity. They identify maleness only with mental and physical toughness and aggressive behavior. They even have a hierarchy between athletes. The bottom line is that there is an undisclosed but dominant idea of manhood for these emerging adults. So, I ask you, How would you have answered

INTRODUCTION

those questions and why? It's definitely a window into the male psyche, don't you agree? It reveals our society's male constructs, what it means to be male, and how we have been influenced in our depiction of the masculine.

There are some truths in what these young men identified in their emerging masculinity, but looking below the waterline, they realized that it was problematic to marginalize other men who don't fit their rubric. Being confronted with that idea, they realized that there was space for the techie, the marching band member, and the golfer at the table of masculinity.

This book is about touching the souls of men in their maze of masculine confusion, where the network of false narratives has emasculated their true male identity. It will help you think critically about what you believe and why concerning your masculinity and its power, and it will bring hope and freedom. You shouldn't have to settle for a cheap, fake version of masculinity.

We have bought into a worthless imitation of masculinity, an impostor, and we are finding it difficult to identify true, genuine, powerful masculinity. It has caused us to go down the wrong road with incredible repercussions to ourselves, those we love, and society at large. Fake masculinity shows up in behaviors we display, thinking they are male, like macho behavior or being emotionally detached. We often focus on the belief that weakness is exposed when we're not able to do something on our own. There is no strength in this version of masculinity—only weakness.

True masculinity is not deceitful or distant. It is authentic and aligns with reality, openness, and responsibility. It's the real deal, not an imitation. True masculine strength is found in the courage to confront our fears, to lay down our lives for others, to live an honorable life, to be honest, and to stand in the gap for justice. Being a man means being responsible, learning to lead ourselves, choosing integrity, and influencing others, honorably leaving a legacy worthy of emulating.

We will take a hard, painful look at what we have embraced in our quest for masculine affirmation. We will unashamedly call out and awaken the brave that resides in us to confront the fears that dominate us and to rise up against the incorrect cultural narratives, which have come to us from other men, women, religion, or current, social, or childhood wounds. The difference between fake masculinity and true masculinity is how it is used. Fake masculinity is toxic, restrictive, and exclusive; the true version is vulnerable, open, and supportive. Either our male power is used for good, or it is destructive. They both have power, but how that power is unleashed, and why, are the crucial components of true masculinity.

We will learn to lead ourselves, to forge male virtues while making brave decisions and distinguishing impostor masculinity from authentic masculinity. What deeply brings us meaning as men is when we protect and provide through sacrifice and bravery, when we uphold what is right over wrong, and when we live out our lives with honesty and vulnerability. These are noble, they represent our power, and they have influence and impact. This book will help you to live in your true masculine identity and harness your masculine strength to bring good to all of humanity.

"When you see the genuine you don't deal with the fake anymore."

—NIMA DAVANI

PART 1

STEP INTO THE ARENA

The unknown outcome in the arena will always be scary, but step into your fear you must, for that defines brave.

CHAPTER 1

THE FORK IN THE ROAD

> Two roads diverged in a wood, and I—
> I took the one less traveled by,
> And that has made all the difference.
> —ROBERT FROST, "THE ROAD NOT TAKEN"

LIFE CONSTANTLY GIVES US FORK-IN-THE-ROAD CHOICES. MOST OF us choose the well-traveled road because we know the less-traveled road will be difficult, unfamiliar, lonely, and painful at times. The bottom line, though, is that the fear of failure stops us from choosing this road. It isn't crowded on this less-traveled road, but when you meet a fellow traveler, you instantly have solidarity and camaraderie. You know each other. There will always be two roads, and the choice of path is yours. Both have a destiny. Which will you choose?

Choosing to go out for wrestling was a fork-in-the-road moment for me. Fifty out of five hundred men in my high school chose the road of three-hour grueling practices five days a week while at the same time losing weight. That's tough, but our wrestling motto was, "It is better to have wrestled and lost than to have played basketball!"

This commitment to train my body, my mind, and my emotions built pillars of self-respect, self-image, leadership, self-control, and bravery. I learned to respect myself when I realized I could push beyond what I thought I could handle, without quitting. I began to see myself as a fighter from within, someone who perseveres. I became resilient, learning self-control by mastering my diet, self-leading by taking responsibility for my daily routines, and bravery by overcoming my anxieties and fears. Fear fears the brave.

Taking this less-traveled road prepared me for every Tuesday or Thursday night, when I had to step in the fear arena and onto the mat to grapple my worthy opponent. I learned true glory was not simply in winning but in crossing the edge and entering the grapple. It was the defining quality that separated the dross from the silver, the true from the false, the brave from the cowardly. Yes, it is in the fire where we are forged, and that's a good place to be—at least after the forging. I continue to lean on these pillars in all areas of my life. They have held me up through a great deal of turmoil, adversity, and hardships through the years, as you will see, and I believe they can do the same for you.

THE POWER OF FEAR

> "For some individuals, fear can be so paralyzing that they are unable to collect their thoughts or even make a move."
>
> —DON MANN, *FACING YOUR FEARS*

Your life will either rise or fall based on constant fear-decision dilemmas. Fear has become a dominating force in American culture.

In her article "Why Americans Are More Afraid Than They Used to Be," Lily Rothman quotes Barry Glassner, author of *The Culture of Fear*: "'Part of what I find interesting about this is that overall most Americans live in what is arguably the safest time and place in human history,' Glassner says, 'and yet fear levels are high, and there are many, many fears and scares out there.'"[1]

Bisma Anwar, in the article "How to Handle Social Anxiety in College," found that current research data concerning social anxiety at the university in "one study indicates that 25.8 percent of college students struggle with social anxiety. Of those: 47.2 percent had mild social anxiety symptoms, 42.3 percent had moderate social anxiety symptoms, [and] 10.5 percent had severe or very severe social anxiety symptoms."[2] Anwar is right; I deal with it every day, story after story, as I'm involved with students from different universities in the Big 12, Big Ten, and SEC.

Fear can control every aspect of our lives. Its power is deadly because it works under our radar, hidden. It tells us insidious lies about who we are and what we're capable of. We must become aware of the lies fear tells us and then call out our brave to slay it by refuting the lie with truth. As we all can attest, our negative, toxic self-talk is both destructive and debilitating.

Recently, a young man confided in me that he was accused of sexual misconduct. His self-image was devastated because it was a lie, and the rumor was going viral within his community. I told him he needed to confront the woman and the lie, to stand up for himself and his integrity. It was his fork-in-the-road moment. But he was paralyzed and wouldn't do it. His choice was to not say anything and trust that it would just slowly disappear. The thought was that, if he stood up for his honor and integrity, it would escalate the drama. He was dominated by this fear and chose not to enter the arena. Once again, I challenged him to call out the brave within him, enter this fear arena, and stand up for his self-worth through talking to her. Sadly, he did not respect himself enough to fight this fear for his self-honor. It was painful for me to watch him choose to not slay his fear. Like many of us who can relate to his fear, my friend simply did nothing. When we let injustice slide, it burrows deep into us. Accumulating this bottled emotion has serious repercussions for us.

His story represents more of us than we want to admit. We are silent, no one knows, and every time we do this, it's like the frog in the kettle: the temperature slowly increases

"It is a timeless truth that many of the things we worry about never come to happen. But our imaginary fears can have real consequences. Fear will cloud your reality, and like other extreme emotions such as anger, will cloud your vision and obscure what is really going on. The grips of fear can be paralyzing."

—RYAN HOLIDAY AND STEPHAN HANSELMAN,
THE DAILY STOIC

until the frog boils to death. Fear does that to us, but we are oblivious of its power and consequences. Wake up, men, to the slow boil.

The young man's imaginary fear obscured his vision and reality. The grip on him was paralyzing. To be honest, I have been in that fork in the road between a fear and facing it, and I'm sure you have too. I've won some and lost some battles against my own imaginary fear. The more I journey on the road less traveled, the stronger I have become. I don't judge my young friend for choosing the well-traveled road; I just want to stand beside him and encourage him. And in this book, I hope to point out the less-traveled road and share what happened to me and why I left the more-traveled road.

When we allow our fears to control and dominate us, it weakens our masculinity. It has a neutering effect that erodes our self-respect, self-discipline, self-confidence, self-leading, and bravery. We must come to understand the power of fear and its control over our lives. Identifying the thing you're afraid of and then defeating it has incredible transformational power.

> "Named must your fear be before banish it you can."
> —(YODA) MATTHEW STOVER, STAR WARS: REVENGE OF THE SITH

"Be fearless. Have the courage to take risks. Go where there are no guarantees. Get out of your comfort zone even if it means being uncomfortable. The road less traveled is sometimes fraught with barricades, bumps, and uncharted terrain. But it is on that road where your character is truly tested. And have the courage to accept that you're not perfect. Nothing is and no one is—and that's OK."

—KATIE COURIC, COMMENCEMENT ADDRESS, WILLIAMS COLLEGE, 2007

We must learn to confront the fears that dominate and control us, that lead us to live cowardly, powerless, dysfunctional lives. Fear causes us to live in bondage, as captives, resulting in our uselessness and irrelevance. The fight begins when we stand up and both name and confront the fear, because fear is powerless before the brave.

Nelson Mandela once said, "I learned that courage was not the absence of fear but the triumph over it. The brave man is not he who does not feel afraid, but he who conquers that fear." Being brave is always a choice.

We are afraid of not being loved and accepted the way we are, of not measuring up to some masculine rubric or a certain standard set by society. We are afraid of being lonely, of not being able to provide and protect, of losing, of being weak, of others' opinions, of being judged, of not being liked or invited into the group, of being gossiped and slandered about, of losing respect from our children, of not making the right decisions, of rejection from either men or women, and ultimately, that our life didn't matter, had absolutely zero impact, and that we might as well have never been born.

That fork in the road, when you decide to either call out your brave or submit to your fear, is always the most consequential. It is the choice that determines everything. When we identify and acknowledge the fear that controls us, we begin the process of dismantling it. To be brave means we uncover a path through the fear.

THE THREE FEAR ARENAS

Brené Brown, in her book *Atlas of the Heart*, states, "In the research, you can find many lists of what elicits fear in us. The items range from rodents and snakes to the inability to see our surroundings, to observing our children in peril. However, no matter how much the lists vary, one item is on every list I've seen: the fear of social rejection. We can never forget that we experience social pain and physical pain in the same part of our brains, and the potential exposure to either type of pain drives fear."

The lessons I learned on the wrestling mat apply to more than just wrestling with a physical opponent. Every time I face an issue that triggers a fear response in me, I visualize it as a fear arena I must enter.

When you identify your fear, walk into your fear arena—you have to face your fear without knowing what the outcome will be. In that moment, you have chosen to call out the brave within you. Your objective when you step into that arena is to kick fear's ass—to defeat the fear that has held you captive.

> "Difficulty shows what men are."
> —EPICTETUS

Now begins the hand-to-hand combat. The arena is where you'll exchange blows, where you'll get bloodied and potentially knocked down. This is where you will feel pain as well as successful triumph. All of this represents bravery, your courage that could not be summoned until you walked into the fear arena. Its power came into being at that moment, where before, fear ruled. In reality, your courage is unlimited, and you can keep calling it out because it has a million different looks and strengths.

If you're used to avoiding things that trigger a fear response in you, then you'll have to learn how to enter the arena and fight. Don't worry, though. You'll learn quickly as you go. In my view, there are three distinct fear arenas we must enter over and over throughout our lives: relational, professional, and private.

Relational fear arenas involve those we love: our family, our significant other, and our friendships—both platonic and romantic. Relationships can be the most volatile, have the deepest hurts and misunderstandings, and can be the hardest to repair when trust is broken. We usually have unrealistic expectations in these relationships, and those expectations have a sabotaging effect.

Professional fear arenas involve aligning yourself with the right career that is sustainable and rewarding. How you interpret failure, how you deal with your boss and your colleagues, or simply asking for a raise can all trigger fear, let alone the big decisions such as quitting a job or changing careers.

Private fear arenas involve our interior lives, the parts of ourselves that are so personal we rarely share them with other people. Often, these involve unresolved issues—the hurts and wounds from our past.

In his article "The 5 Biggest Fears of Men," BJ Foster believes they include the fear of failure, of being incompetent, of being weak (or being perceived as weak), of being irrelevant, and of being foolish.[3] We often want to deny that we deal with these fears. In denying them, we pretend they don't own us. We wear costumes to avoid being defined by them.

MASCULINE COSTUMES

Professional wrestlers enter the ring wearing personas, signified by their over-the-top, hypermasculine personalities and the costumes they wear. Likewise, men often put on masculine costumes and personas to define themselves as men according to the popular social standard. We hide behind these costumes and the personas they represent for the purpose of appearing masculine, but they actually prevent us from realizing our true masculine identity. Additionally, each ethnic culture has male costumes they espouse, like the Latino male culture in comparison to the Black, Asian, or White male culture behaviors.

True masculinity involves leading yourself, taking initiative, and imploring self-control and self-discipline—emotionally, physically, and mentally—along the tight rope of balancing risk-taking with your aggressive and competitive nature. Masculinity starts with knowing how to lead and conquer yourself. The difference between a boy and a man is that a man takes responsibility to lead himself daily.

What I'm trying to communicate is that yes, we still are

risk-takers, aggressive, and competitive. There are different degrees of this—a chess player, techie, entrepreneur, rock band member, rancher, farmer, retail store manager, artist, and cello player can be aggressive and take a risk. When we succumb to fake masculinity, the little boy rules in us and fails to grow into a masculine adult. He doesn't have self-control or self-discipline.

Being a man is calling out courage over our fears, choosing to be responsible, and taking ownership of our decisions. It involves the commitment and determination to do what's right, regardless of the outcome, rejection, or opinions of others. It means taking initiative. It is deciding to persevere with grit and resilience in our hard times and against the adversities of life. It means willingly accepting the painful choices of selflessness and sacrifice. Finally, it means choosing vulnerability, which keeps us honest, humble, trustworthy, and approachable. These qualities give us meaning. This version of masculinity releases its power through these choices, permeating every relationship we encounter. There is nothing fake about these characteristics. They exemplify honor and garner respect. This is the masculine road less traveled.

Masculine costumes allow us to hide from those difficult aspects of being a man, to put on a front of fakery. They come in a variety of looks and styles, but they commonly include a fear of intimacy, a fear of vulnerability, a fear of failure, and a fear of social rejection. Costumes promote becoming something we are not; they cover the true self. The persona is on stage. We deeply value affirmation from other men regarding our masculinity, as well as from women, and the costume can provide this needed affirmation.

> "And, after all, what is a lie?
> 'Tis but the truth in masquerade."
> —LORD BYRON, *DON JUAN*

Let's see if this masculine costume concept reveals how you display your masculinity. Here are a few of the most common costumes we wear:

The athlete: You believe your athleticism and grueling discipline confirm your masculinity.

The power broker: You believe the position of power that you wield over others, decisions, and events reveals your masculinity.

The dominator: You believe you must dominate every situation and person, thinking this proves you are the alpha male.

The mansplainer: You believe that, to be masculine, you must be right in every situation, and if you're not, you lose the man card.

The muscleman: You believe your muscles prove you are masculine—more muscle, more masculine—and you take the 'roids to prove it.

The motorhead: You believe what you drive—the truck, sports car, or brand-name luxury vehicle—defines your maleness.

The soldier: You believe that defending and putting your life on the line, as well as fighting, is macho.

The stoic: You believe men should never show emotion, that it is a sign of weakness and of the feminine.

The controller: You believe men must make all the decisions and be in control of everything, proving the masculine.

The bad boy: You believe that being that bad boy is an expression of the masculine.

The sexual conqueror: You believe your masculinity is tied to sexual conquests and that women or men desire you for it.

In his book *The Masks of Masculinity*, Lewis Howes discusses how these masks are counterproductive: A mask of materialism ultimately leads to emptiness. A mask of stoicism or constant humor hides a deep fear of vulnerability and authenticity. They all hide something deeper that undermines the brave within. They represent the fake impostor.

Of course, I love driving my truck, and somehow, in my male psyche, it makes me feel like a guy. I've been a regular at the gym all my life, I like my muscle, and I was an athlete and coached wrestling and swimming. All of us have several costumes we wear, like the athlete or the soldier. For some of us, that is simply who we are or what we like, and we express it naturally—it's not a costume. But others also take that persona when it's not real. When we choose a costume simply to appear masculine, it really isn't who we are. We are creating a facade, and it will eventually come tumbling down.

There are several problems with this approach. First, you try to be something you are not to prove you are male. You join the military not because of a calling or a love for the mission, but from insecurity or a life without direction. Many come to hate the decisions they make when they hide behind these masks; over time, they realize—maybe subconsciously—that they joined for the wrong reasons.

The bad boy, for instance, performs that role because he defines maleness as being hyperaggressive. Maleness to him means dominating, threatening, and frightening others. The problem is that this persona is harmful to both himself as well as the people around him, which makes it toxic.

In high school, I decided to go out for football based on a lie: sissies don't play football. I bought it—hook, line, and sinker. The last thing I wanted to be seen as was a sissy, which is every guy's greatest fear. So, I went out for football. My decision was based on fear, to prove I was masculine—because I was searching for what was masculine. Well, my first year was terrible. I hated it and only played in one game. That's a lot of practices spent on the sausage squad with no reward. My second year, I became better and played a lot for the junior varsity team. During the summer before my junior year, I had an aha moment, realized what I was doing, and made a better decision to quit. Entering my fear arena, I decided I would not be defined in my masculinity by this sport. I broke the lie I had believed and found freedom, choosing the road less traveled.

We all seek affirmation of our masculinity; we want to be rewarded with the coveted man card. We long for this confirmation. This declaration gives us meaning, purpose, and confidence. It has powerful effects on our male identity and ego.

I was seeking it through participating in a sport. In reality, my masculinity was revealed when I took responsibility to lead my life, chose to call out courage against the fear of being labeled a sissy, and chose to be honest and humble about the reason I went out for football. I felt empowered as I chose the road less traveled and stood up against the social norm of defining my masculinity through a sport. This was a valuable lesson for my emerging masculinity. Additionally, but in a lesser sense, I learned tons from two-a-day practices, pushing myself physically, and not quitting during the season. I also formed connections with other boys going through the same fire that have influenced my maleness.

Is our masculinity defined by an external costume, or is it defined by something internal? Have we pursued the wrong thing in our quest to fulfill our maleness? What will it take for you to take off the costume and reveal your true self? That act may just be the most courageous decision you will ever make. It requires vulnerability, honesty, and humility.

The unknown outcome in the arena will always be scary, but you must step into your fear—that defines and forges a brave man. When we allow our fears to control and dominate us, it weakens the masculine, having a neutering effect. When this happens, it erodes our self-respect, self-discipline, self-image, self-confidence, our ability to lead ourselves, and our bravery. We must come to understand the power of fear and its destructive and controlling influence on our lives. It causes us to live cowardly, powerless, dysfunctional lives as captives, resulting in uselessness and irrelevance.

Over and over throughout our lives, we must enter those three distinct fear arenas: relational, professional, and private. And I have found that the fear of social rejection permeates all three. Men often put on masculine costumes and false masculine personas to define themselves as men according to the popular social standard. We hide behind these costumes to appear acceptably masculine, but they actually prevent us from realizing our true masculine identity.

The fight begins when we call out the brave that lives within us, when we stand up and confront the fear, because fear is powerless before the brave. You must identify the specific fear that brings out your cowardice, call out courage, and commit to stepping into its arena and fighting, knowing it's a fight that will involve a grittiness of never giving up or giving in. You must get back up and learn from the knockdown, stay focused on the goal, and fulfill your God-given purpose. This is more than a single fight; it's a revolution. In a revolution, you become the solution to the problem. You model the behavior for all to see and emulate.

BRAVEASS REFLECTION

- Fear has the power to control our lives. We must learn to identify and dismantle our fears. How has the power of fear controlled your life?
- Name three fears that have plagued you and consider why.
- We must learn to remove the masculine costumes we hide behind. What masculine costume do you wear, when did you put this costume on, and why did you choose this costume?

CHAPTER 2

THE RELATIONAL FEAR ARENA

Where fear is, happiness is not.

—LUCIUS ANNAEUS SENECA

THE RELATIONAL FEAR ARENA INVOLVES OUR INTERACTIONS WITH the people we love: our family, our significant other, and friends. All relationships involve clashes, struggles, disagreements, and conflicts. Unrealistic expectations can destroy the relationship or keep us from working through conflict toward a resolution. Fear is often the reason we choose not to enter a relational conflict.

The decision to live with current relational pain usually trumps the decision to conquer the conflict in a relationship. We become paralyzed, many times because we fear the person's response to our honest communication. Ultimately, that person controls us, holding power over us. Healthy relationships involve degrees of trust, transparency, honesty, understanding, and vulnerability. Entering this fear arena will require the courage to address the hurt and to clear up misunderstandings with the person. You will need to be honest, humble, transparent, and vulnerable and must be able to listen to and understand their responses. Neither of you is perfect. Entering the arena can deepen your relationship, creating a bond built on honesty and openness. This too can be scary because you place yourself in an opportunity to be rejected.

It's scary when you're emotionally vulnerable because you may be attacked, and the outcome you desire may not happen. It's also scary when the person wields power over you—say, in withholding acceptance or becoming angry, mean, or emotionally detached. But it's worth entering this fear because it has the possibility to strengthen and make the relationship better than what it was. You break the power and become free, create deeper intimacy, and build trust and loyalty. And it sets you up for future healthy dialogue. Remember: happiness and fear never coincide; it's an illusion to think differently.

Relationships involve connections and intimacy with others. There is no deep connection without honesty. They influence how we feel, think, relate, and behave with each other. Trust, honesty, and vulnerability are foundational for healthy connections. We all have a need to belong, to fit in or feel like we are accepted and a part of the group. It affects our emotional and

"Problems call forth our courage and our wisdom; indeed, they create our courage and wisdom."

—M. SCOTT PECK,
THE ROAD LESS TRAVELED

mental health. It affects our happiness and how satisfied we are with life.

Belonging can only occur when we are transparent and honest about who we are, standing beside our imperfections and our needs, offering our true genuine self to others. The depth of belonging is proportional to the vulnerability we offer each other. Our acceptance of ourselves has an amazing influence on others. They respect it because they are struggling with accepting themselves.

Our deepest hurts come from our relationships, as do many of our deepest joys. I have found this fear arena very difficult to enter because of these truths.

For many, family relationship conflicts may have been swept under the rug for years, adding to the difficulty of dealing with them. And then you have family secrets that no one ever talks about because of shame. As a teenager, I found out my dad's twin brother had a previous marriage and a secret son; this situation was never discussed. I remember wondering where they lived and whether they had met anyone on our side of the family. In my house, it was like they never existed; no one was in contact with them.

Many families tiptoe around the elephant in the room for decades, but at what cost? These elephants might include siblings who hate each other and have no relationship, a gay or lesbian son or daughter, sexual misconduct, depression, addiction, conflicting political views, and conflicts between spouses, to name a few. The power dynamics can be hard to navigate.

However, the truly healthy relationship you can create by

THE RELATIONAL FEAR ARENA

bravely entering this arena and defeating the relational fear is absolutely worth it. Restoration is possible by embracing healthy and honest behavior toward each other. It's easy to simply give up and live with the hurt, shut down, emotionally detach, enter protection mode, or start blaming. I can vouch that I have used many of these coping mechanisms, especially choosing to give up, live with the hurt, and emotionally detach. In any relationship, it's common for people to be hurt, misunderstood, judged, and accused, and we often arrive at wrong conclusions or create false narratives when we fail to communicate honestly with the other in our relationship. These outcomes can be emotionally overwhelming and damaging. No wonder healthy relationships take wisdom, understanding, listening skills, constant communication, clarification, selflessness, patience, and insight from each partner. Most relationships require a lot of courage and humility to break through the fear to build trust, intimacy, friendship, and love through beginning—and continuing—the difficult conversations.

In this chapter, you will learn how to successfully enter the relationship fear arena by identifying and dismantling relational fears, identifying and choosing honesty with humility, and taking ownership of your part of the relationship. Authentic relationships require you to strip off your masculine costume.

Entering this arena may be extremely painful, which is why many are debilitated by fear or choose not to enter. We aren't sure we'll be able to manage what will happen if we go in.

> "The chief task in life is simply this: to identify and separate matters so that I can say clearly to myself which are externals not under my control, and which have to do with the choices I actually control. Where then do I look for good and evil? Not to uncontrollable externals, but within myself to choices that are my own."
>
> —EPICTETUS, TRANSLATION FROM *THE DAILY STOIC*

THE RELATIONAL FEAR ARENA

It's always a mystery, and you can't control mystery. You have no idea what will rise to the surface in these situations. Obviously, fear creates lots of scenarios in our mind that heavily influence our emotions, telling us it's too dangerous to start the conversation.

We have no idea what will happen when we enter the relational arena. We cannot control the other person, but we can control our choices and our attitudes. We can choose to enter the fear arena of relationships both to create intimacy and depth of friendship and to resolve conflict and hurt. And regardless of the outcome, we take solace that we made the brave choice to value intimacy. That choice garners strength and confidence within our soul.

When you enter the relational arena, in respect to conflict resolution, there is an outside chance that you won't reach a resolution. Realize when you enter the fact that no one is perfect; we all have issues, and it takes two to tango. In the conversation, you might be confronted with the ways you've been wrong or with how you've contributed to the demise of a relationship. You might learn something that will challenge the victim narrative you have composed to keep you safe and apparently perfect. Of course, all of this can also be true for the person you were in the relationship with. The point is that entering the arena doesn't always end with you as the victor, but the fight—and the potential for fulfilling relationships—is worth the risk.

In order to enter the arena, you must choose to let all of that go and to prioritize the survival of a relationship above being right, which can be a struggle of its own. You must enter knowing you cannot control the other person. You enter for the possibility of restoration. The bottom line is that it's a risk, and risks often come along with fear because you do not know what the outcome will be.

I shared with a friend a relational conflict I was having with a coworker. In the conversation I distinctly remember saying, "But I'm right, and he is wrong." My friend's answer was, "Well, what is more important—to be right or to salvage the relationship?" It took me a few days to make the decision to give up being right in order to avoid destroying the relationship. I have a strong sense of right and wrong and justice, but I can also be arrogant, so it took me some time to confront my ego and pivot my approach. But I have been in countless situations where this scene has occurred again in my life, and I've coached many men in the same dilemma.

We feel disappointed when our relational expectations are unmet. I must constantly remind myself that humanity is broken and imperfect. And that includes me. People's choices, decisions, emotions, and behaviors are out of my control. I can only control my attitude, choices, and emotional responses.

Part of stepping into the arena is being honest with yourself and others. This is frightening because you have zero control over their response to your honesty. Over a decade ago, I committed infidelity, betraying my marriage vows. It was a devastating mess for my wife, children, friends, and of course myself. Intimacy vows are rooted in love, forgiveness, respect, vulnerability, trust, and honesty. When infidelity is exposed, the one cheated on is emotionally tortured and humiliated. This spills over onto the children. My wife divorced me, lots of friends left me, and I lost the Christian community I was involved in. Stepping into this personal fear arena meant owning and taking responsibility for my actions, choosing to go to a therapist, and reinventing myself.

I learned the following painful lessons from this train wreck:

- What true friendship is and isn't
- That my actions have consequences far beyond what I could articulate or imagine
- How to walk through pain and let it be my mentor
- What it is like to be abandoned, rejected, and hated
- The nastiness of shame—both from others and from myself
- That I cannot control other people's reactions or the narratives they create about me
- To let it go, forgive, and control my responses to others' hatred, judgment, and anger toward me
- To understand grit and resilience and to never give up or give in
- To reclaim and reinvent myself
- To forgive myself and be compassionate and kind to myself, acknowledging I'm not perfect
- To realize that humility has great power

- To realize that I can't change yesterday, but I can change today
- The amazing dichotomy of living with pain yet living my best life

Thankfully, I have had an incredible therapist the last nine years. She has been instrumental in leading me through the process of deep reflection with insightful questions. I would have never been able to come up with this path on my own. She spoke truth into my self-hatred and sabotage, and she provided incredible insight that implied it wasn't all my fault. She helped me learn how to deal with the lack of forgiveness and the punishment imposed on me. Additionally, a few incredible men never left me and have been involved with me in this journey, along with my sisters and their husbands. An aspect of love is that it simply shows up. Love does not judge, reject, or abandon. Love does not insist you change, follow certain rules, or compromise. You always have a seat at the table, regardless of everything else. A true friend never leaves you in your darkest hour but rather joins your fight, willing to share your fate. I had a few who did this, but the majority did not. As it says in Proverbs 17:17, "A friend loves at all times: a true friend will not only love when it is easy, but at all times."

The difficulty that impedes your direction *is* the direction. Once you come to terms with this reality, you push forward with grit and allow the internal forging to remake you. Hopefully, some of these lessons can give you hope if you have been in a similar situation or can help you avoid my mistakes.

THE RELATIONAL FEAR ARENA

A thirty-year-old friend named Zach, who I mentor, grew up in a home where both parents were drug addicts. That's not the best of environments to be raised in. His childhood was not normal, and he became an adult at an early age. After leaving home, he invited his dad to come live with him in a desperate attempt to help his dad get sober and back on his feet. Zach entered his fear arena bravely and nobly, to love the unlovable, to sacrifice his time, emotions, and finances.

He entered into his deep pain of the dysfunction of his childhood by choosing not to abandon his father, hold a grudge, or remain unforgiving. Instead, he embraced what little his father could give him and became the father instead by providing unconditional love and wisdom while his dad acted like an adolescent, a man child. Zach was the victim but chose to deny his pain power over him. He rose above in his actions toward his father. Most young men in this situation would simply refuse all contact with the dysfunctional dad, become bitter and angry, and bury the emotions that come with not having what he deeply desired—to simply be a son and have a dad to take care of him. He entered his father wound through accepting his dad, keeping the conversation going, providing shelter and food for his dad, being the only support his father had, and speaking truth and wisdom to his adolescent father.

I and others provided a safe place for him to dump his emotional pain, spoke truth about the situation, and gave counsel and affirmation. His character grew from doing what was right among all that hurt. Zach realized that it wasn't the family dynamic he wanted, but it was a relationship.

Unfortunately, his dad died of a drug overdose a few years later. It's not the ending he desired for his dad, but because he entered his personal fear arena with his dad, he lives without guilt of leaving him. He continued his relationship with his father instead of ending it, and his children got to know their grandpa. He learned to love unconditionally, and he served his father and did all he could do to help him. Zach also has beautiful, indelible memories of his dad's words telling him he loved him and was proud of him and his accomplishments. He taught Zach the male value of fiercely protecting his kids and those he loved and of being responsible. His dad said the same quote every time they parted: *Catch you on the flip side!* One day, Zach will catch him on the flip side.

As Marcus Aurelius states, "Look well into thyself; there is a source of strength which will always spring up if thou will always look." His strength amid deep pain humbles and guides me. I've learned and have been inspired by my friend to be a better man. His masculinity spoke to my masculinity, and my masculinity spoke to his.

Here are six things I would share about my journey on entering this relational fear arena:

- You cannot predict the outcome—drop all expectations when you decide to enter the arena.
- You must decide to initiate, call out your brave, and step into the fear—there is no other path.

THE RELATIONAL FEAR ARENA

- It is the beginning of the journey—its length at this point can't be determined, and you're in it for the long haul.
- Humility, apology, and saying you're sorry may be required.
- All sorts of negative emotions will surface, like self-hatred, self-condemnation, and shame.
- Pain will probably surface, but for the first time, you can work through it and become well.

I like what Victor Frankl said in *Man's Search for Meaning*: "Everything can be taken away from a man but one thing: the last of the human freedoms—to choose one's attitude in any given set of circumstances, to choose one's own way." When it comes to relationships, you choose your own way. I chose my own way and I like what I have chosen. It hasn't been perfect, but it's been right, and it has blessed me.

Syndicated columnist Ann Landers writes, "If I were asked to give what I considered the single most useful bit of advice for all humanity, it would be this: Expect trouble as an inevitable part of life, and when it comes, hold your head high. Look it squarely in the eye and say, 'I will be bigger than you. You cannot defeat me.'" This is the kind of attitude that leads to a resolution. Commitment and determination move you into healthy relating.

To enter the relational fear arena, you must choose to prioritize the survival of a relationship above being right. You must be willing to forgive after you have been wronged and deal with hate while not holding a grudge. You must realize you cannot control the other person. You enter for the possibility of restoration. It's a risk, and risks always come with fear attached.

We will constantly feel disappointed when our relational expectations are unmet. I must constantly remind myself that humanity is broken, imperfect, and unpredictable. I can only control my attitude and choices. Our deepest hurts come from relationships, and I can't control other people; I can only control myself. Remember: it always takes two. The other person may be committed to hurting you by refusing to reconcile. Bitterness and hate are justified by them, as they are determined to punish you. When we harm someone, it's cruel, but we must realize we also harm ourselves. The bottom line is that, if we return the hate and bitterness, then we are no different than they are. Let go of it. Hope that they will see their hate and its effects on those around them, as well as its acidity on themselves as they become bitter and mean. Your brave must surface and overpower your fear to restore a fractured relationship. You must learn to listen and acknowledge fault. And if there is a wrong narrative circulating about you, you must enter that fear arena by standing up, respecting yourself, and speaking truth.

Joining the revolution will mean you will grapple with relational fears by entering the relationship arena with family, friends, colleagues, and significant others. Sure, it will be awkward, scary, and at times very emotional, but it's the only path to make things right. Taking action will unleash your masculine power.

BRAVEASS REFLECTION

- Our deepest hurts come from relationships. Can you describe some of your relationship hurts?
- Is it more important to you to save a relationship or to be right?
- Your brave must surface and overpower your fear to restore a fractured relationship. What would this look like for you?

CHAPTER 3

THE PROFESSIONAL FEAR ARENA

Of all the liars in the world, sometimes the worst are our own fears.
—RUDYARD KIPLING

FEAR KEEPS YOU FROM YOUR DESTINY—IT STEALS YOUR FUTURE. Professional fear can come from a variety of sources, ranging from how you interact with those you work with to asking your boss for that long-overdue raise. Overcoming the fear and entering this arena may require making difficult and stressful life decisions. It may even require reinventing yourself professionally or choosing a different career path. It's crucial that you learn how to be uncomfortable when necessary, how to navigate the toxic peer energy that often dominates work culture, how to deal with your boss, how to interpret failure, and what it looks like to reinvent yourself.

EMBRACING DISCOMFORT

I was a paper boy at ten, worked on the road crew in high school, and cut, raked, and bailed hay on the Kansas prairie. This was my work experience until after college. These jobs taught me responsibility, hard work, and endurance—true Kansas values—and helped me pay for college.

When I was a paper boy, one customer wouldn't pay me until after delivery, meaning I had to pay for the papers myself. This pissed my dad off, and one day, he said, "Get in the car. We are going to go talk to him." I remember being super scared and not wanting to go. We drove up to the house, got out of the car, and went to the door. When the man appeared, my dad proceeded to ask him why he wouldn't pay me, a ten-year-old little boy, when my payment for the papers was due. Well, a huge argument ensued and ended with my dad saying, "Why don't you come out of the house onto the street, and I'll settle this with you man to man?" The man's wife screamed and slammed the door shut. I had never seen my dad get angry, cuss, and instigate a fight. I love this snapshot of my dad. He showed me a picture of masculinity and standing up to fear. He was protecting his little boy, regardless of what could happen. His sense of injustice spoke out; he confronted this man's power over a little boy who was powerless and brought his power to the situation.

He made me feel safe and loved. He fathered me well that day. But guess who had to go back the next month on collection day? As a ten-year-old, I had to go up to that man and ask for my money. It was scary, and it was the last thing I wanted to do. I dreaded it because I had no idea what would happen. But I pushed through the fear by walking up to the door each month to collect my pay. Interestingly, his wife always answered the door and paid me. I never saw the husband again. That one decision has been foundational for the rest of my life. It taught me that I could overcome my fear and that I should always maintain my self-respect.

NAVIGATING TOXIC PEER ENERGY

In the middle of my professional career, I had a conflict with a colleague. I was his boss, and I have a strong, confident, charismatic personality, which I have found can be threatening to some people. My colleague suffered from depression, and he struggled with jealousy and a poor self-image. These issues eroded our relationship and caused conflict. I asked him to seek counseling, but he refused. I felt like I was always walking on eggshells when I was around him, always trying to lift him up and encourage him. This became consuming and burdensome because it never created a chance for him to change. I felt like I was beating a dead horse. Part of the issue was that he didn't like who he was, his design, or his skill set. He also felt like a failure. My issue was arrogance and the need to be right.

We brought in the counseling team from the nonprofit organization we both worked for to initiate a conflict resolution. They listened and gave us suggestions, and we listened to each other while we each expressed our frustrations, apologized for anything we had done to hurt each other, and put together a plan to move forward together. This was very beneficial for our relationship and for the work environment.

I believe the keys were vulnerable listening and seeking to understand so trust could be reestablished. We each chose to self-sacrifice and put the other's interests above our own. We decided that our relationship was more important than being right and considered how we each interpreted events differently and why. We chose to support each other and promised that, if an issue came up, we would immediately discuss it to get clarity and understanding. These truths upgraded our working relationship.

He was also asked to get a counselor and work on some deeper issues that were significantly impacting him. Sadly, he refused. We entered this professional fear arena together, but he didn't have the courage to address his own personal fear issues. That would mean admitting something is wrong. As men, many of us refuse to admit something is wrong because we believe we need to be invincible, that we must always have the answer, and that strength means never being needy. Sometimes this confession is made difficult by the fear of what we will find out. Will we be able to keep it all together, or will we completely fall apart? Unfortunately you can't get past that fear without working through it. For many men, the mentality is that the problem is out there somewhere, it's because of somebody else, and we never take personal responsibility or accountability to look at ourselves.

DEALING WITH BOSSES

In reference to bosses, I fortunately have had some incredible bosses who have believed in me, let me lead without micromanaging, affirmed me, and supported growth and development by sending me to conferences. These bosses are easy to affirm and follow and support. One such boss is Rudy. I always want to go the extra mile for him.

I have also had bad bosses who lacked integrity, honesty, and camaraderie. That behavior creates a toxic work environment and may mean you hate coming to work. These bosses rule through command and control, not through creating trust. They lead through threats, making you fear them. Their power is in the fear they wield over you. Realizing this and making a choice to walk into this fear arena by disagreeing, stating your opinion, or questioning decisions is scary because you don't know what their response will be, or you have already seen or experienced an angry, demeaning, or unethical response.

This is a rough spot, especially when unethical and immoral decisions are being made. But you must call out your courage, enter this professional fear arena, and challenge the unethical decision; by doing this, you also stand by your own values of right and wrong. Another choice involves wisdom. It may be wiser to keep your mouth in check and control your attitude. When I've been in this situation, it's a daily grind, and I must start my morning routine with prayer and commitment to keep my focus clear when the toxicity boils up.

These fear arenas show up in the fear of being fired, marginalized, ridiculed, or labeled. It might also be a fear of a curtailed career, where you never get a promotion or a raise. It takes incredible integrity to avoid being like such a boss. Choosing the road less traveled is tougher because many times your peers aren't on this road—you're alone. The following decisions helped me in these difficult situations: I can only control my choices and attitudes; I need to fulfill my responsibilities and try not to enter degrading conversations; I must control my anger because it will not prove valuable (except in cases of abuse, where anger may be appropriate). My morning routine of centering myself is crucial to all of these.

Your boss can belittle you, but they still can't control who you are on the inside. It will require more courage each day in this arena, courage to speak up for a raise or to defend yourself if they are power-dominating you. Oftentimes we go to work knowing there will be a confrontation following up on something that happened the day before. Before walking into work, I have to get myself in the right head and emotional space.

The rituals I do to get into this space are helpful. First,

I think through the scenario I might be in and how I would respond. I do this before the discussion so I won't be caught off guard. Next, I ask the boss questions for clarity. I need to make sure I understand the situation and what my boss wants from me. Then, I am simply responsible for doing my job well. Finally, I reflect on my part of the interaction. I journal on what it is about this boss that drives me crazy and then take a hard look at the cause. I ask myself whether it might be triggering an event that happened earlier in my life. I often reread my journaling before going to work or at lunchtime. I also ask myself what I am learning about myself and about good and bad leadership.

The bottom line is that a hostile environment can be an extremely difficult place to work. Spending the majority of your day in this type of culture is draining. It can be difficult to maintain your performance without sinking into an attitude of bitterness and compliance. If it continues to be toxic, move on when you can. At times, I have had to stay in the job because of the economy or personal situations, and at other times, I quit.

FAILURE

Most of the time, I don't get it right the first time. I fail. That used to bother me, but now I'm over it, for the most part. I regroup and stop the self-degradation and rise again. I usually get it right on try number two or three or ten. I evolve from failure into success. I love Thomas Edison's take when

> "The greatest glory in living lies not in never falling, but in rising every time we fall."
>
> —NELSON MANDELA

he was focused on inventing the most commercially viable light bulb: "I have not failed. I've just found 10,000 ways that won't work."

For many, their concept of failure is warped, and because of that, failure is seen as bad. Men incorrectly judge and condemn themselves for failure, and it becomes something to be avoided at all costs and to be kept a secret if it happens. When I failed in certain areas, I felt incompetent, and I hate feeling that way. My condemning inner voice wants to label and harass me. It goes back to my guidance counselor telling me my senior year of high school that I'd never make it at Kansas State; it was too rigorous. By the way, I made it and went on to get a master's degree at the University of Nebraska–Lincoln. Grit supersedes intellect every time.

> **"Develop success from failures. Discouragement and failure are two of the surest stepping stones to success."**
> —DALE CARNEGIE

My wrestling coach taught us to learn to fail forward: to let it move us forward in our goal. In *Failing Forward: Turning Mistakes into Stepping Stones for Success*, John C. Maxwell states, "The difference between average people and achieving people is their perception of and response to failure." Many label themselves as a loser because of their failure. It smashes their self-esteem, self-confidence, and self-respect. But I have seen it do the opposite for me many times. Failure is a mentor. To grow means you take risks, and you make mistakes and then recalibrate and try again. And bravery is the catalyst.

I failed in starting my own health and fitness company. I had a few customers, but it never took off. But I learned a lot. The big lesson was that marketing is everything. I failed in another venture with a partner training corporate leaders and writing articles on culture. It didn't fly, but I walked away with deeper insights on culture and training, and I became much better at writing. Sure, it was discouraging, especially all the time that was put into it, but the failure moved me forward.

When I was fired in 2008, the economy went into the Great Recession, and I could not find another job. It was a double whammy for me emotionally. For me, it wasn't the Great Recession but the Great Depression.

I went from a six-figure income to poverty. I moved to the sketchy side of town. When someone asked me where I lived, and I told them, they said, "Aren't you scared?" My response was, "Well, my people go to your part of the city to steal; we don't steal from each other." My new community taught me how to apply for food stamps and assisted utilities. Talk about a Humpty Dumpty experience! It took incredible energy just to get out of bed in the morning.

I was trying to start a new life, but I had no idea where to start. I found myself constantly heading in the wrong direction and having to recalibrate. I set up daily goals of how many jobs to apply for, how much time to work out at the gym, and how much time to read and journal to keep me sane. My emotional and mental wellness needed to be my priority. This was a lonely, grueling time that seemed to have no end, dragging on year after year. When I couldn't find a career job for four years after being fired, it took determination and commitment to keep going. Albert Einstein said, "There is only one road to true human greatness: the road through suffering." Man, have I been on this road for a lifetime!

During that stint, I became resilient. I trudged forward. It was a long and winding road, leading myself emotionally in my attitudes and discipline every day. I committed to applying to five jobs a week and to finding work to survive. Emotionally, it was a roller coaster, and I had to learn to take control of my emotions and not let them control me. There were good days and bad days, but I didn't give up. Three times, I was curled up in the fetal position, sobbing and screaming at God—four years is a long time. I journaled and read spiritual books, as well as leadership and self-awareness books. These gave me strength and purpose in the midst of chaos. I placed my hope in trusting God in this long darkness. I did my best to conquer the day and to remain grateful along the way. I thought about all I had learned in being a wrestler and transferred it to this current situation. My grit became stronger. My determination was to stay the course of my long-term goals and to not give in or give up during this hardship.

REINVENTING YOURSELF

This shattering of my professional life rocked the self-image I'd gained from successes and accolades throughout my twenty-seven-year career. It affected my sense of identity and self-worth. Being in a space where no one knew me or my achievements was humbling. Reinventing myself professionally has been a long, hard road, and there was a steep learning curve. I made massive mistakes, but I never gave up. I kept entering the damn fear arena and throwing my punches. It took four long years of searching, four long years of weekly rejection until I finally got my first breakthrough. Louis Pasteur said, "My strength lies solely in my tenacity."

In her blog post "Reinventing Yourself: 10 Ways to Realize Your Full Potential," Shonna Waters says, "Reinventing yourself means identifying patterns, values, or activities that no longer serve you and changing them for better options. It can involve external characteristics, like a job, hobbies, appearance, relationships, and location. True reinvention also happens inside, in how you think and behave. It will be different for everyone, which is what makes it so powerful."[1] Reinventing yourself professionally will require the following.

First, you need to take a long look in the mirror so you can become self-aware of who you are at this stage in your life. I'll never forget an indelible moment with a counselor in Jacksonville, Florida. She pulled out a mirror and gave it to me and said, "Look into this mirror, John, and ask yourself, *Who are you?*" This literal reflection showed me that I wasn't living up to a commitment to values I said I believed in. I was a fake. I didn't know my true self. In reality, I didn't know who I was at all. I was a mess, but now I could at least see it. This was a beginning to a new journey, a decision to take the road less traveled. We all need to be willing to evolve, and there needs to be a commitment and excitement to start all over.

Second, you need to leave things behind. Let them die, and bring forward only those things that will fit into who you want to become, like values and virtues. For example, I put to death my religiosity but brought to life a new spirituality.

Third, you need to start molding and reshaping yourself. This often requires new training or development. You must be mindful, with a learning and inquisitive spirit. Many times, you will start at the bottom and bust your butt and keep advancing until you have made a name for yourself. You must prove yourself worthy in your leadership, integrity, competence, and skill set.

Finally, you need to give it moxie!

This is a tough phase. You will feel twenty-five again—but not in a good way. Moving your way up is even tougher if you were at the top of your game and are now entering a game you've never played before. But if you continue to climb, you will achieve little breakthroughs. One thing that kept me motivated was that I loved who I was becoming. I felt aligned with my purpose, why I was created, and complete. Understand this isn't a fast track. Usually, it's a slow track. Stay gritty; it might have lots of up and downs. Continue to be a learner and push through.

> ## "The man who moves a mountain begins by carrying away small stones."
> —CONFUCIUS

I found work at $9 an hour as a ramper at an airline that kept me just above total poverty for a year, and then I continued the career search. I was in my midfifties. My career consultant advised me to take dates off my résumé so potential employers wouldn't know my age and to subtract years of service to avoid age discrimination. By this time, I realized I wasn't being given the same opportunities a younger person would be given, but I was determined not to give up. And yes, that killer statement—"You're too qualified for me to hire"—can be devastating.

In my pursuit of reinventing myself, I decided that, since I couldn't find a job, I would add to my education. I got accepted to Cornell's online Human Resource certification. It provided a goal to pursue, keeping me focused. I also decided to enter a bodybuilding contest to give me a focal point and keep me disciplined. I worked at gyms and as an assistant swim coach during the day, and I was a bouncer at a bar at night to pay for food and rent. It was a hand-to-mouth existence. I had seen poverty from living in Zambia and Uganda, but for the first time, I was living in it myself. It definitely shook my faith; I remember numerous times cursing God.

> "I will either find a way or make one."
>
> —HANNIBAL, CARTHAGINIAN GENERAL

My first breakdown was in year two, followed by more setbacks. It was like drowning, coming up for just enough air to breathe, and then being pulled back under.

AUT VIAM INVENIAM AUT FACIAM

This quote and the story of Hannibal motivates and speaks to me. So many times in my life, this is my trumpet call. Your mantra needs to be the same as Hannibal's: "either find a way or make one."

Remember my story about being a wrestler? That experience helped me to not give in to my emotions and fears when facing the toughest challenge I'd ever endured. I had to go to an even deeper place because it was about survival now. I had to decide not to give up. I was being reformed and reforged in the fire, painfully hammered out.

And I was so alone in this process. Pain was mentoring me, and I had become intimate with it. I never want to experience that again, yet it was one of the best experiences in my life. From my journaling and reading leadership and self-awareness books, I was able to reshape my calling. I was called to develop, counsel, encourage, lead, and empower men, giving them value and blessing them.

I wanted to get back into higher education but by a more traditional route. I got my first breakthrough when I accepted a position with Kansas Campus Compact as their assistant director. My job was to use my mentoring skills and experiences to put together a program to increase retention for incoming freshman, many of whom were first-generation students. My master's degree from the University of Nebraska–Lincoln was in educational psychology, and my thesis was in mentoring. I would be working at eight different colleges and universities in Kansas and based out of Kansas State University. The starting salary was $30,000. It would be the most I'd made in four years since losing the six-figure job. I packed everything up, left Denver, and headed to Kansas. I'd made it through the desert. I was entering the next phase, excited yet knowing this was just a stepping stone. I had found a way, and up next was creating a way to reinvent myself.

After working for Kansas Campus Compact, I moved into a different aspect of higher education. I soon learned not to trust peers or bosses so quickly. I kept getting burned, and there was an ugliness of not wanting me to gain power or reputation, so I was denied certain natural moves upward. It was painful. But in the middle of this, I had one of the best bosses who believed in me and gave me full rein to lead. Interestingly, though, as time marched on, those less-trusting bosses were removed, and I started gaining a reputation for my calling, passion, and skills, and I took their positions. Recently, I accepted one of my dream jobs.

I learned invaluable lessons during those twelve years that forged me into who I am today. The iron needed to be brought to a high temperature to cull out the impurities. Of course, refining who you are is lifelong, but those years are indelible. To reinvent yourself, you must answer the following questions:

- Why should you reinvent yourself?
- What will it demand of you?
- Write out your expectations. Are they realistic?
- Who will be on your team to ask questions, give advice, and check in with you every three months on your progress?
- What are your yearly and three-year goals in respect to reinventing yourself?
- When you hit a goal, how will you celebrate?
- Do you really believe you can do it?
- Will you be able to be a learner in the process?
- Can you be patient enough?

The professional fear arena speaks to lots of situations and issues in the workplace, ranging from how you interact with those you work with to asking your boss for that long-overdue raise. It may require reinventing yourself professionally, choosing a different career path. It involves how you interpret failure, how you deal with your boss, your attitude and communication tone, your willingness to be uncomfortable when necessary, and your ability to navigate the toxic peer energy that often dominates work culture. In signing up to be involved in the revolution, you will need to overcome your fear, enter the professional arena, and learn to navigate work and career relationships.

BRAVEASS REFLECTION

- It will take courage to stand up for yourself, and you will need to get comfortable with being uncomfortable. What does this mean for you?
- Regardless of bad bosses or peers, you control your attitude and decisions. They don't have that power. Don't hand your well-being over to them. How will you ensure you lead yourself in this situation?
- Change your perspective on failure: fail forward, and let it teach and change you. Journal on why failure can make you your best.
- Reinventing yourself will not be easy and can even be discouraging at times, but it will be worth it. Keep moving forward. How do commitment, determination, hope, and patience affect reinventing yourself?

CHAPTER 4

THE PRIVATE FEAR ARENA

He who has overcome his fears will truly be free.
—ARISTOTLE

THE PRIVATE FEAR ARENA IS UNDOUBTEDLY THE HARDEST ONE TO enter. Private fears involve our interior lives, the parts of ourselves we rarely share with other people. Often, this includes shame and unresolved issues from our past. These are our secrets, and secrets have power. Understandably, we fear rejection. We decide to be alone because we are afraid of being hurt. This is an internal fear we deal with every day—alone. These struggles can seem bigger than life and insurmountable because we are so alone with them. Many of us compartmentalize these events to survive.

Renowned shame researcher Brené Brown defines shame as "the intensely painful . . . experience of believing we are flawed and therefore unworthy of acceptance and belonging."[1] Certain communities shame us, and people tell us we are flawed, not accepted, and can't belong because of who we are or what we have done. We all face rejection and abandonment, and it has devastating effects on us. And we take the shaming from those others and use it to shame ourselves. We buy into the lie. We spend our lives disguising and covering up our shame. It is in control. We just want to hide because we don't like who we are because of what happened to us or what we have done. When shame entered, everything changed. Shame replaced self-acceptance, self-love, self-blessing, vulnerability, and courage, and regaining these virtues is the way to defeat shame.

You may ask, *What is the difference between guilt and shame?* Guilt stems from doing something bad; shame looms from the belief of being bad. With guilt, I ask for forgiveness because I believe I did something wrong; with shame, I believe I am what is wrong. Shame causes people to feel defective, unacceptable, and damaged without repair.

SHAME FROM TRAUMA

The source of our shame could be sexual, emotional, or physical abuse, often by someone we trusted. It could involve family violence, addictions, refusal to conform, or verbal toxicity. Sometimes it derives from religious community standards of what is acceptable or, of course, things that we regret

THE PRIVATE FEAR ARENA

because of not living up to our own virtues and inflicting pain on others. Whatever trauma is the source of our shame, we are committed to keeping it a secret.

If the trauma occurred at a young age, we're more likely to have drawn incorrect conclusions. As children or adolescents, we don't have the cognitive or emotional bandwidth to process trauma with maturity and may mistakenly believe the abuse was our fault. These wrong conclusions latch on to us and follow us into adulthood. This is an incredibly scary arena, full of confusion and hurt.

According to *Psychology Today*, "Trauma is a person's emotional response to a distressing experience. Few people can go through life without encountering some kind of trauma. Unlike ordinary hardships, traumatic events tend to be sudden and unpredictable."[2] It is also important to remember that "traumatic events can have deleterious effects on health at any age."[3]

An adolescent trauma for me was when I saw my dad get into an argument with my mom. In his rage, he started strangling her and dragged her into the bedroom, putting a .45 pistol to her head. That's trauma I can still visualize today. It was brutal. When this happened, I frantically went to the phone to call the police, but in that split second, I couldn't do it.

My faulty reason, fear, and fragile self-image told me that, if I made that call, it would alert the whole town to the chaos and dysfunction in our home. Our family name would be ruined. It was the fear of social rejection. I weighted the fear of this outcome and its consequence in favor of the safety of my mother. This is another picture of shame: we must keep it hidden, keep the secret no matter what the cost. I didn't start talking about this until my midforties.

For decades, I beat myself up over this decision. I was ashamed that fear, social rejection, and self-image ruled me. I hated that I didn't stand up but cowered instead. It was a measuring stick I used against myself. Decades later, I came to realize three things:

- that a little boy should have never been put into that situation,
- that you can't let isolated events label you, and
- that my conclusions from the event were wrong.

I thought for years that it was my fault, that I was a coward, and that I always made wrong decisions. Even today, it is difficult at times to share this painful event because of people's opinions. Every time I tell the story, I look fear in the eye. My therapist, Kristine, guided me through this wound. I read lots of self-awareness, shame, and abuse articles and books, as well as talking to fellow travelers on this road and friends who simply listened. Kristine also had incredible insights to share with me. The combination was a catalyst for my well-being today.

We must let trusted friends or a professional into the secret for it to implode and for healing to begin.

Shame plays a vital role in the personal fear arena because it causes us to hide. We have spent a lifetime disguising and

THE PRIVATE FEAR ARENA

covering shame up, but still, shame takes control. We just want to hide because we don't like who we are after what happened to us or after what we have done. Shame replaces self-acceptance, self-love, self-forgiveness, self-blessing, and courage. We usually bury these ugly events, thinking that will take care of them, but you can never bury anything alive. It's just a matter of time before it will surface. Something will trigger the event later in life. You must pursue and be completely committed to its death to ensure your complete freedom. You must get a good therapist to help you unravel deep hurts. I challenge you to choose to join the revolution and grapple with this fear, forbidding it to define you and affect every relationship. The greatest revolution is fought and won in the heart. You must be resolute to want to get well. Perhaps the truer definition of a hero is one who takes responsibility to heal their own wounds and then shows others how to do the same.

BRAVEASS REFLECTION

- Shame causes us to hide. We disguise, cover up, and pretend. You must come out of hiding by talking about it with another. It is the only way to put it to death. How can you make a commitment today to destroy it?

- Many times, our interpretation of a traumatic event when we were young is wrong and plagues us into adulthood. How would you describe the event today as the thirty, forty, fifty, sixty-year-old you?

CHAPTER 5

TAKING YOUR LICKS

> The world breaks everyone, and afterward,
> many are strong at the broken places.
> —ERNEST HEMINGWAY, *A FAREWELL TO ARMS*

IN ALL THREE OF THESE FEAR ARENAS, YOU WILL GET KNOCKED DOWN over and over again. The key is being able to get back up, acquire wisdom from the knockdown, change your strategy, and keep punching. This is how you will learn to be resilient in the face of adversity, how you will grow from taking your licks. Transformation only happens when you enter the fear arena. No one is transformed while standing on the outside of the arena or sitting in the stands watching. Entering your fear arena is your defining moment. Every time you enter a fear arena, it will demand that you identify and name the fear you are dealing with. Then, you must call out your brave so you can make a decision. Without the brave, you make the wrong decision. Now, make a choice to step into the arena. Finally, begin the fight. You must walk the talk.

NAME THE FEAR

When you name the fear, you give yourself a known target. That fear might be rejection, abandonment, loss of respect, fear of asking someone out on a date, an undesirable outcome, marginalization, being misunderstood, or needing to own up to something. It might include others' anger and its manipulation, social rejection, being disliked, losing control, or losing a friendship or loved one. Whatever it is, now you know it, and you can face it.

CALL OUT YOUR BRAVE

Call out your brave by reminding yourself when you were brave before or visualizing what the brave will look like. Think of how it feels to be in the arena, facing your fear. You must be honest. Visualize what it will look and feel like to be a coward or be scared, and confront that feeling. Next, visualize what it looks like to be brave and strong, to be free. You can't get well by ignoring, and you can't live in freedom when you run away from your own darkness.

TAKE CONTROL OF YOUR NEGATIVE CONVERSATIONS WITH YOURSELF

Take a few days and simply record what you are saying to yourself. Why are you saying this, and where did this destructive thought come from? Is this statement true or false? You must take control of your thoughts because they are part of the fight. You must replace these negative thoughts that affect your emotions, decisions, and behaviors with truth. In *Unfu*k Yourself: Get Out of Your Head and into Your Life*, Gary John Bishop said, "Create the reality you want to live in by beginning the process of having the kind of conversations (with yourself and others) that actually shape that reality."

MAKE THE CHOICE

Now make the choice to step into the arena. We all have courage in us, but we lack the understanding of how to call it out. You call it out by stepping into the arena, by walking your talk.

FIGHT!

Fighting occurs in your head. Your emotions will do battle between your negative, destructive self-talk and your truth talk. It occurs in the dialogue you have with someone, listening and standing up for yourself, and it may occur in taking action to initiate or control your attitude with others' offensiveness and selfishness.

The ability not just to fight but to keep on fighting is a crucial skill. You can learn how to build it by facing up to adversity, allowing yourself to establish authentic and supportive relationships with other men, taking ownership of your mistakes, and asking for help. You must become gritty, never give up, and stay the course. Men who lack resilience become weak in the face of adversity; they fold. Simply put, don't just tap out.

EMBRACING ADVERSITY

No one gets a free pass. Adversity is a fact of life. We have all been broken in some way or another. We all have regrets, we all have made stupid mistakes, we all have made bad decisions, and we all have had embarrassing moments, but in spite of this, we must get back up and make great efforts to be honorable. With adversity comes pain, suffering, bewilderment, fear, and frustration. For some, it brings life to a screeching halt, and for others, it forges a life of resilience. As Benjamin Franklin said, "The things that hurt instruct." When suffering, pain, shattering, and the hardships of life happen, some are defeated and discouraged, but the resilient become strong in the face of adversity.

Our lives are full of adversity. We get one problem taken care of, and along comes another. They are never-ending. We have a decision to make every time adversity comes along. We can choose to enter the fray, call out the brave within us by making a decision, and leave fear behind. We punch adversity every time we decide to act. In many cases, it is lots of combined actions.

For example, if you lose your job, you either allow discouragement to rule you, becoming paralyzed and unable to move forward, or you call out your brave and push through the pain of the adversity and put together your résumé, use your networking system, and start applying for jobs. With this action, you overcome your fear and its emotional drama that takes space in your mind and heart. You must face the fear of how you will pay the bills and the mortgage, how you'll provide everything the kids need. Fear immobilizes you with its imaginary conclusions. You must act with courage to dismantle the fear of your imaginary conclusions.

Otherwise, we can run away and give up like cowards. We must brave the journey; we must face the ordeal. It gets bloody and messy when you choose to step onto the mat, and no two fights are the same. The common denominators are fear, courage, determination, and a persevering attitude. Find your brave. There are no other choices. Sometimes I get my butt kicked, and other times I kick butt. But endurance and perseverance are a must because we can't control the timetable.

To be honest, some of my fights have lasted for decades. For example, with my dad, I chose to constantly move toward him, work at understanding him, give him mercy and grace, and forgive him. I took him out for lunch, watched movies with him, played golf with him, and asked him questions about life. When I did this, it gave him respect and honor, and it was a slow healing, a process of ups and downs, especially with my attitude. Remember from the scriptures that "suffering produces perseverance; perseverance, character; and character, hope" (Romans 5:3–4).

Being an athlete in high school, I learned indelible character traits from football practices twice a day in the Kansas heat, hungry wrestling practices from cutting weight, and two-hour track and field workouts. I was a broad jumper, a runner in the medley relay, as well as a hurdler. I also learned discipline from being a saxophone player. Self-discipline, not giving up, hard work, self-control, and being pushed beyond what I thought I could handle forged these invaluable virtues at a young age. As I state earlier, I have called on these skills numerous times throughout my life. I also took lots of licks during those years and learned a lot.

During the Great Recession of 2008, I was let go from a six-figure, twenty-seven-year career, got divorced, and my mom and dad died six weeks apart. I was knocked out and beaten down. My new reality revealed that life can be very harsh at times. The heat suddenly intensified more than I had ever experienced, and I was in the crucible, with the dross separating from the silver. In these combined purifying events, a new man was being shaped. The Herculean struggle is where we define ourselves.

When this happened, I had a choice of either being defeated or getting up and reinventing myself. I had to take the fight to my greatest enemy, my fear. It was rough, a good 9 on the Richter scale of stress. In my twenty-seven-year

> "A crucible is, by definition, a transformative experience through which an individual comes to a new or an altered sense of identity."
>
> —WARREN BENNIS AND ROBERT J. THOMAS, "CRUCIBLES OF LEADERSHIP," *HARVARD BUSINESS REVIEW*

career, I had accomplished a lot of good things—led some incredible initiatives, engaged in some successful endeavors, worked hard to establish myself, maintained an honorable reputation—but then they all became meaningless. Needless to say, it was a difficult place to be at my age. It was a painful and heavy burden I needed to bear. I had to let go of my reputation—my identity—and move into the unknown while becoming unknown. I had to identify and pursue a new purpose. You rebuild and reclaim your life by renewing your sense of purpose. That was my Mount Everest! It takes a lot of trial and error during the climb, hitting plateaus and then focusing on the next climb until you finally summit. It's a long, arduous climb. Those high school lessons from football, wrestling, track, and playing the saxophone served me well decades later.

With my parents passing, I constantly carved out moments to let myself grieve the impact of not only their relational loss, but also the loss of long-standing traditions that occurred at their home. I grieved with my siblings by talking about our parents: the good, the bad, and the funny. We listened to each other and what we were feeling in the loss. My mom was both of my sisters' best friend. I grieved my parents' wisdom, their unconditional love, their words of affirmation, their support, and their conviction of the significance of family. There are times I speak to them. You learn to live with the pain but not let it control you. You can have joy and sadness at the same time.

ATTITUDE

Attitude was key. It can either be an asset or a liability. Negative attitudes are destructive and divisive and bring nothing to the table for change and healthy connecting. A negative attitude may be a result of not working through hurt. Hurt people hurt people. They involve anger and resentment, self-defeating self-talk, pessimism, and complaining.

> "The greatest discovery of any generation is that a human being can alter his life by altering his attitude."
> —WILLIAM JAMES, AMERICAN PHILOSOPHER AND PSYCHOLOGIST

Positive attitudes move us in the direction of hope, change, and encouragement. Jennifer Okafor says, "The definition of a positive attitude encompasses a state of mind that allows you to envision and expect good things. It does not mean living in denial of the negative situations around you. A positive attitude means allowing yourself to stay optimistic. The benefits of a positive attitude include anticipating happiness, health, success, and opportunities and, in turn, keeping top of mind the positive outcomes that you may want for yourself."[1]

Additionally, The Mayo Clinic claims that positive thinking and optimism affect overall health in many ways, including longer lifespan, enhanced immunity against diseases, a healthier heart, and improved stress management skills, among other advantages.[2]

> "Nothing can stop the man with the right mental attitude from achieving his goal; nothing on earth can help the man with the wrong mental attitude."
> —THOMAS JEFFERSON

I developed a daily ritual with getting my attitude squared in the morning through reading, reflection, and journaling, and when I hit the pillow at night, I review my day and thank God for each event, carving an attitude of gratefulness.

RESILIENCE

Remember the famous picture of Mohammad Ali's iconic knockout punch against Sonny Liston—the victor standing over the vanquished? It was a harsh conclusion to a short but brutal fight. That is exactly how I felt. Within a year I was financially destitute, living in someone's bedroom, on food stamps, and giving plasma to survive. I was emotionally devastated from losing my mom and dad, who knew me the best and had loved me the longest, and now felt orphaned as all traditions in their home ended. I held my mom and spoke into her ear, comforting her as she died, and then six weeks later touched and talked to my dad as he died. I had never been with anyone as they died. It was the most painful and yet most sacred, holy moment I've ever experienced. Life for me would never be the same as before because of these four devastations of getting divorced, losing my job, sinking into deep poverty, and losing the two people who had known and loved me the longest. I will never be that man again because of the suffering. I cannot undo what happened.

But I became a stronger man in all the broken places. Resilient people integrate what happened to them; the experiences become a part of hammering out a different person. You must allow the suffering to do its work rather than running from it or pretending it isn't there. It shapes you differently because you must take responsibility and own a mistake instead of being irresponsible and blaming others. You become a man of character. It's the only path to forge deep beauty of character.

Authenticity comes through the beating and hammering as you're vulnerable and honest with your life's narratives. The man resurrected from his death is humble, understanding, compassionate, and wise. He gives lots of room for others' failures, realizes there is something behind the curtain when others are angry, and gives them space with both a deep sense of confidence and a secure self-image, self-worth, and hope. I'm learning to simply be kind because I do not know what another is going through. Trust me—I have good days and bad days during this transformation. We are all in process.

Many of you can relate with my hardships, but others could add the harshness of a friend's or family member's suicide; the loss of a child or a sibling; the judgment of others; emotional, mental, and physical abuse or assault; rejection or even abandonment from your family or a family member; or the constant shaming from other people. Up to 90 percent of us will experience at least one serious traumatic event during our lives.[3] Resilience is the ability to withstand, overcome, grow, and continue the journey.

I was not born with resilience. No one was born with it. We are never prepared for these tragedies, misfortunes, and life-altering trauma. We become resilient people while we navigate these difficulties, learning to endure the pain and suffering and being resolute in our trial as we walk through the devastation and rebuild. Some painful experiences we will never fully recover from. We simply learn to carry the pain, holding it throughout life yet not letting it control life. This is another picture of resilience.

In his book *Resilience: How We Find New Strength at Times of Stress*, Frederic Flach identifies resilience as disruption and reintegration. I feel like disruption and reintegration have always been a part of my life. How about you? Can you relate? The key is learning how to reintegrate.

Like many of you, I have had to carry lots of emotional pain. I make choices to become intimate with the pain instead of hiding from it, pretending it is not there, running from it, medicating inappropriately, or letting it conquer me. I become a person I didn't know when I'm intimate with the pain that emerges.

> "Resilient people turn fear into courage, suffering into strength, and pain into wisdom."
>
> —ERIC GREITENS,
> *RESILIENCE: HARD-WON WISDOM FOR LIVING A BETTER LIFE*

To be intimate, I become close and connected with the pain and loss. It is a practice that leads to healing and healthiness. I weep, I mourn, I grieve, I get angry, I pray, I reflect, I journal, I scream, I cuss at God, I accept, and I feel. Closeness emotionally, mentally, physically, and spiritually in the crucible of resilience shapes a stronger, wiser, more understanding person. I rise and reclaim, and I reinvent and move forward. It doesn't mean the pain is completely gone; it means I call out courage and stay in the fight, bruised but standing, then healing and becoming strong. Most of life is out of my control, and I needed to allow the process to do its work. It's not done yet and won't be until I die.

The poet Lord Byron stated, "Adversity is the first path to truth." Resilient people find meaning, purpose, and growth in the difficulties. They learn to hold out against, prevail over, and grow from the experience. They find truth they never knew or experienced.

There is no victor without a fight. Hail to the resilient ones.

Steven M. Southwick and Dennis S. Charney, in their book *Resilience: The Science of Mastering Life's Greatest Challenges*, identified that the resilient people they interviewed exhibited the following shared factors: "Confronted their fears, maintained an optimistic but realistic outlook, sought and accepted social support, and imitated sturdy role models. Most also relied on their own inner moral compass, turned to religious or spiritual practices, and found a way to accept that which they could not change. Many attended to their health and well-being, and trained intensively to stay physically fit, mentally sharp, and emotionally strong. And most were active problem solvers who looked for meaning and opportunity in the midst of adversity and sometimes even found humor in the darkness. Finally, all of the resilient people interviewed accepted, to an impressive degree, responsibility for their own emotional well-being, and many used their traumatic experiences as a platform for personal growth."[4] I have found truth in these resilient factors, and it was powerful when I read their findings years later. They confirmed I'm resilient. I'm proud of that. It's one of my defining virtues.

ASKING FOR HELP

We often do not want to ask for help, to appear burdensome or needy. Shame causes us to wear a constant mask of independence. Larry Hagner from *The Dad Edge Podcast* identifies seven reasons we don't ask for help.

- "We think we can do it all by ourselves.
- We are scared what others think of us.
- We're ashamed of where we are in life.
- We don't want to lose our reputation.
- We have a fear of judgment.
- We fear rejection.
- We don't want to face the truth of ourselves."[5]

These reasons tag us, don't they? And they can have a compound effect on us where two or three feed off each other and shut us down. We hate admitting we need help. The lie we believe is that needing help equates to weakness. What man wants to be seen as weak?

We all want to be Superman. He's always strong, saving the day, never needing any help. But we aren't Superman. Somewhere along the way, we bought into the lie that a real man always knows the right answer, is totally self-sufficient, always saves the day, and never needs any help. That's an unattainable expectation, and it is destructive and toxic. It introduces us to failure, depression, self-doubt, and anxiety. A big issue is asking for emotional support. We refuse to do this, and it has mental and emotional repercussions on us. We believe it shows weakness and shame, and we fear appearing broken or needy. We often do save the day, showing our masculine strength, but many times we don't do this alone. We need other Supermen. And if we ask for help, we become better heroes. To be honest, not asking for help is weakness, not strength. Those who refuse to seek help are cowardly.

Asking for help needs to become a part of our personhood. Asking for help provides real benefits. When I ask for help,

- I become real,
- I connect with other men,
- I step into vulnerability,
- I become courageous,

- I become wiser,
- I acknowledge reality and that I'm not perfect,
- I give a death blow to my toxic ego,
- I become approachable,
- I gain camaraderie, and
- I win.

Asking for help involves first identifying who you trust enough to approach about your need. Then you must call out your brave by opening your mouth and asking. You must accept the truth that you are not alone in your need. Then, debunk the negative self-talk that stops you from deciding to ask for help. Finally, choose to put your emotional, physical, and mental wellness first.

OWNING YOUR MISTAKES

We all make mistakes; it's part of being human. There is no one on the planet who is perfect and always makes the right decisions. What separates boyhood from manhood is taking responsibility and owning our mistakes. This requires honesty, humility, a controlled ego, and a secure self-image. Thomas Merton said, "Pride makes us artificial and humility makes us real." Everyone desires these values in a man and in his leadership because they elicit trust and respect, but these values are seldom seen. The price is too demanding for most. Many men define masculinity as never being wrong and

"The leader must own everything in his or her world. There is no one else to blame. The leader must acknowledge mistakes and admit failure, take ownership of them, and develop a plan to win."

—JOCKO WILLINK AND LEIF BABIN, *EXTREME OWNERSHIP: HOW U.S. NAVY SEALS LEAD AND WIN* always knowing what to do. They lack the courage to be honest and to take responsibility and admit when they make a mistake, which is the true picture of the masculine. Instead, we blame others or make excuses. We assign the mistake to somebody else, taking ourselves off the hot seat. We are not at our best when we hide, blame, and accuse others of our bad decisions. Guilt rots us from the inside.

We have become a blame culture. As Daniel Lobel put it in an article for *Psychology Today*, "Blame is the act of assigning responsibility, but they are not the same thing. In addition to assigning responsibility, blaming is designed to find fault. . . . A fault is a defect . . . whereas taking responsibility is not a sign of defect, but rather a virtue."[6]

And Todd Henry, in a podcast episode titled "Dealing with a Culture of Blame," suggests that a large portion of this "blame-shifting" is to safeguard ourselves from looking like failures, which can negatively impact our employment, relationships, and well-being. Since no one wants to look like a failure, we do whatever we can to avoid this label.[7]

No one wants to take ownership of their decisions when they are wrong because of the condemnation and judgment that may come pouring down on them. Blaming involves assigning the responsibility for something bad onto someone else. If this has ever been done to you, you know it's infuriating.

Society's standard is perfection, which is unattainable, and it is a setup for both failure and for blame. This expectation of perfection is especially relevant for leaders and for men. It is a vicious cycle. One small scent of blood and the pack of wolves come in for the kill. It's mean, hateful, and cannibalistic. Holding men to a standard of perfection is a current blight on our culture. This unrealistic standard means no one wants to take ownership for fear of being crucified. Blaming is just another form of hiding, and the reason for hiding is fear—the fear of being invalidated as a leader or a man and disrespected.

When we come to that line-in-the-sand moment of deciding to take ownership, to be responsible and accountable for our life and our mistakes, we are keenly aware of the price. That is a sacred moment for every leader and every man. This sacred moment is a ritual of letting go of the unrealistic expectation that to have influence as a leader or a man, you must never make mistakes, and then rising into something better. It is about accepting that you are fallible, that you will make bad decisions that can have a deep impact on others, and that you are not right all the time. That's living in an authentic place.

Recently, a friend who is smart, handsome, and athletic made a mistake. He was on a date, and he got super drunk because of his insecurities in relating with women. He was embarrassed and felt very guilty for his behavior. But he took responsibility for his actions and apologized to his date for making her night miserable. He owned his behavior instead of making an excuse. He asked her to give him another chance and took her out to a nice restaurant, where he told her that he struggles with anxiety around women, and that's why he got drunk. He simply had a glass of wine that night, and they got to know each other better. I have found what James M. Barrie said to be true: "Life is a long lesson in humility."

My friend didn't run from his mistake; he faced it, was humble and apologized for it, and asked his date to join him in moving forward. This is what maturity looks like. There is a deep peace that comes in this place, a deep confidence surpassing understanding, and a humility from honesty that takes root, but most of all, there is freedom. When you accept responsibility for your actions, you'll be free from other opinions and judgment, and you can more fully become your own man. It allows you to rise up. It brings strength and power and conviction, and in some mysterious way, it protects you.

A huge part of manhood is taking ownership and being responsible and accountable for your life, your career, your family, your significant other, and those around you. Owning our train wrecks will require vulnerability, and vulnerability is not for the fainthearted. It just might require the most courageous acts you have ever taken.

Owning your mistakes requires strength of character. When you own it, you make a decision to be honest, and honesty requires being vulnerable. When we do that with our significant other, our children, friends, or our coworkers, we ignite our masculine soul. For me, owning involved acknowledging that I committed adultery to my wife, kids, relatives' friends, coworkers, and religious community. I needed to change my behavior and be willing to get counseling. And I needed to surround myself with men who could speak truth and join me in this dark time in my life.

Nothing in my life has been more humbling and painful as when I chose to admit I committed adultery. That was vulnerability on steroids. Every time I own this, I always fear some people will judge me—and many do or silently distance themselves. It's always a decisive act to not hide and to be honest when I choose to be vulnerable.

My reputation was compromised; many had no desire to reestablish it because as a leader, I had broken their trust. Once again, there was a huge price to pay for being honest and owning what had happened. I was in the hot fire of the crucible.

We must choose to correct ourselves and change, have more compassion and understanding, and give others grace and mercy. We must weep over and with those our bad decisions have affected and stand up against those who will still throw their hate, condemnation, and judgment.

When men are responsible and accountable for their actions, it speaks to other men in a powerful way. The strength to stand up and be honest and humble exposes healthy male confidence that, in turn, attracts other men. They will wish to become comrades with the responsible man, stand side by side with him, and be teammates with him, ready to take on any adversity and make an impact on the world.

Recently, I had a team member make a grave mistake involving him slandering another organization because of its wrongful response concerning a case of sexual misconduct toward a woman. What he said was public knowledge, but he used it inappropriately to try to sway a decision. He thought if the client knew the story, the client would choose to eliminate them. But the client had already bonded with the men in the other organization, so he took their side and identified with them being slandered. I received an angry phone call from the client, and we lost the deal.

My sacred moment was upon me. How would I respond? I was upset that we had lost the deal, but I also knew my team member was zealous and highly competitive, and that what he said was spoken in the heat of the moment.

After listening to the client, it came my time to speak. I told him it was my fault, as I was the overall leader. I expressed deep sorrow for what had been said and the damage it caused. I asked if there was anything I could do to make it right and then proceeded to say I was sorry. I asked them to please forgive me and the team.

Next, I met with the team member and told them about the conversation and what I'd said. I knew this was a teaching moment. I talked with the team member about ownership and honesty. We reviewed what it means to lead with integrity. And I told him that he should not have said it but that I knew it was said out of zeal and his competitiveness, that I still believed in him and trusted him, and that we should get back into the game. He acknowledged his mistake, and we talked about how to better handle these situations. I also told him that, ultimately, the buck stopped with me. That I had not done an adequate job in training them to handle situations like this one.

The bottom line is that I wanted my team to know I had them covered as their leader. I would not throw them under the bus. If they had made a mistake, then I had not trained them well enough; otherwise, they wouldn't have made it. The whole event bonded us closer together rather than ripping us apart.

Building resilience requires taking ownership of your mistakes. Why, you ask? Because resilience is hammered out in times of choosing to be vulnerable by being honest and truthful with your mistakes, regardless of what others think or how they react. Your resilience rises when you own your mistakes.

The revolution acknowledges that life will have difficulty and men need to become gritty and persevere, forging the incredible character quality of resilience. We are in this together, and no one gets a free pass. Adversity is a fact of life. We have all been broken in some way or another.

We have a decision to make—we can choose to fight, or we can run away and give up like cowards. We must brave the journey; we must face the ordeal. It can get confusing on that mat, and no two fights ever play out the same way.

> **"We become just by performing just actions, temperate by performing temperate actions, brave by performing brave actions."**
> —ARISTOTLE

No one was born with grittiness. We are never prepared for what life can throw our way. We become resilient when navigating these hardships, enduring the suffering and pain as we survive and rebuild. We will never fully recover from some of our experiences—we simply learn to carry the pain.

Resilience leads to the discovery of meaning, purpose, and growth. Resilient people grow from their experiences and find new truths. There can be no victor without a fight.

BRAVEASS REFLECTION

- Adversity is a fact of life. Resilient people find meaning, purpose, and growth in the difficulty. What have you learned from the adversities that showed up in your life?
- What friends of yours are your true friends, who are willing to stay by your side no matter what?
- We hate admitting we need help; we believe that needing help equates to weakness. What are some of the contexts in which you need help, such as personally, your career, your fathering, being a husband, being divorced, your emotional and mental wellness, or your finances?
- Owning your mistakes requires the strength and bravery to be vulnerable. Is there a mistake you have made that you need to take ownership of and correct?

CHAPTER 6

ANGER ISSUES

> Anger is an acid that can do more harm to the vessel in which it is stored than to anything on which it is poured.
> —MARK TWAIN

GURPREET SINGH, IN AN ARTICLE FOR WELLDOING.ORG, SAID, "ANGER is an adrenaline-fueled, powerful, emotional, and instinctual response that . . . produces a fight or flight [response]. . . . Anger's role is to protect the ego."[1]

In some cases, anger is not bad but appropriate. In a significant conversation on my self-degradation due to being angry, my therapist taught me this truth: You should be angry if you have been violated. It is the right response. I viewed all aspects of anger as bad or wrong, but Kristine said, "John, in some experiences that have occurred in your life, you should be angry for what was done to you. It wasn't right. And in some situations, John, it was cruel and mean." For example, I should be angry that I was asked to start working with students by the dean of students, but the immediate supervisor didn't want me in the equation and was offended that the dean had made the request, so she blocked the process and then resigned three months later, leaving me with nothing. That was cruel and mean; I should be angry for what she did. It was totally unprofessional, and her disregard for what I could bring for success was infuriating.

Anger should call out the courage and strength to stand up for yourself without being mean. Professionally, I needed to let the dean of students know what happened to me. I needed to be self-controlled, factual, and honest. In response to the supervisor, I asked her why she had refused to meet with me. I also told her how I felt that she had blocked my employment and asked her why she wanted to hurt me. As you can image, the conversation was intense. There was no resolution, but the most important dynamic was that I called out my brave in doing this action. I stood up for myself, involving self-respect. These acts of confronting our fear and choosing brave build the muscle of inner strength and self-confidence.

But masculine anger can be brutal. Men can be emotionally and physically abusive to women, other men, their family, and even to themselves when they don't understand their anger. And this can be complicated when they refuse to seek help or justify it as "men being men." We allow anger to conquer us instead of seeing its destructive wake and conquering it. This is toxic masculinity. Anger is used to dominate, control, threaten, and manipulate. The usual recipient of this is women, and of course a man's children. You also see this in the work environment, with peers, and against other marginalized communities.

WHAT IS ANGER?

The American Addiction Centers categorized anger into ways it is expressed: chronic, passive, overwhelmed, self-inflicted, judgmental, and volatile. They suggested that if you experience these categories, you likely have an anger issue and may need help to address it.[2]

Without that treatment, anger can lead to any number of problems. It can damage your health through constant levels of stress and anxiety, and it may harm your relationships with the people around you. It can also be contagious. Uncontrolled, angry outbursts can induce anger in your partner, or it may show your children that it is an appropriate reaction to stress. This can lead not only to them acting out in school or conflict with their peers but also to a nasty cycle of generational anger.[3]

Anger can be expressed in many ways, including the healthy reaction to injustice I discuss earlier. Singh called that type *assertive* anger. The less-productive expressions include *aggression*, where you direct your anger at someone else;

passive anger, which is bottled up for later (when you might explode with aggressive anger); and *rage*, which is uncontrolled, dangerous anger.[4]

LEARNED ANGER

The father has an incredible influential role in how he deals, displays, and manages his anger with his sons and daughters. His sons may naturally follow how their father treated their mom during times of conflict. Was his anger out of control, volatile, scary, and abusive, or was his anger self-controlled?

I can recall, to this day, the major fights my parents had and my dad's out-of-control anger toward my mom. It was ugly. I never saw a resolution to the anger, an act of expressing an apology or an admission of wrongdoing. I was left without closure or exemplification of how to love each other again after a disagreement or major conflict. So, would this be my go-to behavior when conflict occurred in my relationships? It's important for men to recognize where they learned their habits for expressing their anger during conflicts or how to resolve conflicts with their significant other, friends, coworkers, or bosses.

According to Matt Glowiak, from an article for ChoosingTherapy.com, "Anger issues are more common among men with adverse childhood experiences, adult trauma, poor interpersonal functioning, and the presence of mental health or substance dependence disorders. Covering up other feelings with displaced anger is a defense mechanism to protect a deeper vulnerability."[5] It's important to be aware of any factors that might influence what triggers your anger and how you express it. Being aware is the first step to controlling it. Usually, anger is a secondary emotion that is being expressed because of a primary emotion, such as hurt or sadness. So to take control of your anger, you must identify the hurt or sadness and begin at that place. Additionally, I have learned that my anger may be a result of a blocked goal.

By learning the origin of our behaviors, we can begin to deconstruct the emotion. This allows us to think consciously about our reactions and restructure them into a healthier response. When I uncover the hurt or pain that elicits my anger, I must then allow myself to feel the hurt that anger has covered up. It's an aha moment every time for me. The pain or hurt someone had done to me years earlier was now being vomited up on others. They were the brunt of my unhealed hurt with someone else. I've recently been challenged with the thought that when I harm or hurt another, I actually harm and hurt myself. In response to anger being a result of a blocked goal, I now ask myself, "What goal is being blocked, John?" This question has been extremely insightful.

We are a byproduct of the culture we were raised in—not just in our family but all around. We instinctually mimic what we saw and experienced. Some of these behaviors are good, and some aren't. We become mature when we learn to deconstruct and reconstruct the beliefs we were raised with. Then, we can evolve into something better and healthier.

ANGER AS A MASK

Wearing a mask simply creates versions of who you are that are untrue. It's different characters that you perform depending on the need. Wearing a mask is running away from who you are. A few years ago, I was counseling a young man named Jim who had recently gone through a painful breakup. We discussed how he and his girlfriend had argued and how his explosive anger had entered the argument.

Every relationship has problems that need to be worked through, and anger is a significant barrier to resolving those issues. Many men have no clue about where their anger is coming from or how to manage it. Ryan Martin, a psychologist at the University of Wisconsin–Green Bay, put it this way: "Most of the time, emotions are complicated, and we feel lots of things at the same time. For some people, though, it's easier for them to focus on the anger because it feels safer than those other feelings."[6] As I state earlier, anger can be a secondary emotion, meaning that it hides a more painful emotion beneath it. You need to look for the primary emotion that is driving it and deal with that. As I have done this, I have discovered that sadness and pain have elicited my anger.

Carroll Izard, at the University of Delaware, determined that we have ten discrete emotions: interest, joy, surprise, sadness, anger, disgust, contempt, fear, shame, and guilt. I asked Jim to search his feelings and to name which emotions might have been hiding beneath his anger. Some of the emotions Jim identified were sadness, anger, disgust, contempt, shame, and guilt. These emotions surfaced because of being rejected, misunderstood, undervalued, disrespected, and frustrated with his own unhealthy response.

In the midst of our conversation, he was able to see the emotions prodding the anger, and he was able to see that he mimicked his dad's anger. He wanted to have a better, more appropriate expression that wasn't damaging. He realized his anger, contempt, fear, guilt, and shame had caused his girlfriend deep pain, and she wasn't going to accept it. He took ownership of it. He was honest and humble. He apologized and then changed his behavior.

We must dissect the anger and figure out the primary emotion behind it. We must understand why we feel the way we do and which means of expressing our anger are unacceptable. Additionally, it's good for us to explore how we have previously witnessed or experienced anger and are now just mimicking without processing how it was expressed. We must fully acknowledge the devastating effects of our anger on ourselves and those we love and truly desire to change our behavior. This is where we deconstruct and reconstruct.

OVERCOMING TOXICITY

Anger is powerful and controlling, and we know that, so we use it to our advantage to create fear and dominance. It's a mirage, though; in truth, we are scared, fragile, weak, and fearful, and we use the anger to cover up those emotions. For example, many men believe that they must be right, must know all the answers all the time. If we are wrong or unsure, then we must be weak, and no man wants to feel weak. So our anger jumps to the rescue, or so it seems, to protect us.

Choosing to acknowledge being wrong, to be honest, to be humble, and to accept responsibility are masculine and powerful actions. It is a picture of masculine strength, not weakness. We are recognizable as men by our display of character qualities like self-control, humility, honesty, understanding, discipline, self-sacrifice, and ownership. Our masculine strength comes from forging these characteristics. This is where true masculinity lies: in our ability to control ourselves, standing firm in these virtues.

The following are questions all men need to ask themselves:

- Is my outburst of rage making things better in the situation?
- What blocked goal do I have that is causing me to get angry?
- What emotion is below the anger, which is bringing my anger to the surface?
- How do I conquer anger instead of being subservient to it?
- Is there an interplay between my anger, anxiety, self-image, or fear?
- Looking at all aspects of my life, what parts of me are fueled by anger and why?
- When is anger right and appropriate?

ANGER ISSUES

"All great changes are preceded by chaos," as Deepak Chopra said. Change is always difficult, and all of us resist it in some fashion, but it's worth it. Acknowledging my role and seeing its power caused me to rethink my reactions. I learned to be careful with what I say and the way I behave. I have made so many mistakes and hurt countless people by allowing my anger, contempt, fear, and sadness to rule me. It's embarrassing, and I have dealt with a lot of guilt.

The good thing is that it caused me to seek help. I distinctly remember the first meeting nine years ago with my therapist. When she asked why I had come to her, I told her, "I am so angry, and it is spilling out everywhere and onto everyone, including myself." This started my journey to recovery of deconstruction and reconstructing a better John. Identifying and then starting to talk about my deep pain of sadness from several experiences was erupting my anger. My pain was now causing others pain. Interestingly, there was a theme of rejection and abandonment, along with never being good enough and difficulty accepting love.

Who says we don't have emotions? Hell, anger comes pouring out of us all the time. This is a piece of the true man code: we have the courage to look at our hurts and get them healed so that our anger is diffused and we operate from a place of self-control, self-discipline, and integrity. We need to stop running away from our deep and scary emotions and honor them through sitting with them and letting them speak to us. It's assuming responsibility for ourselves, where we lead ourselves. When this happens, we are able to bring peace, calm, love, compassion, and understanding to our relationships. Our masculine power is revealed in our ability to control ourselves and make the decision to heal from the hurt done to us, as well as the hurt we have caused and the hurt we do to ourselves.

The revolution is calling you to leave the toxic side of our masculinity and the uncontrolled emotion of anger and head to a true picture of our maleness and its positive power influencing everyone around us. It's in this space where we shine and bring strength and hope.

BRAVEASS REFLECTION

- Although anger can be used for good, if it is uncontrolled, it can be extremely harmful. How has your anger become harmful?

- Anger can also be learned. In fact, we've all developed reactions based on our families, communities, and society. Can you think back to when you were younger and consider what you learned about anger and how you express it today?

- Anger often hides a more central emotion below it; knowing which is the true feeling can help you address it. What is the painful thing that is triggering your anger?

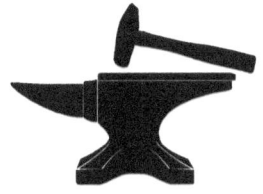

PART 2

WHAT DOES IT MEAN TO BE A MAN?

Change awaits us. What is decisive is our deciding.

—*GREGORY BOYLE, TATTOOS ON THE HEART*

CHAPTER 7

FAKE MASCULINITY

Show me the man you honor, and I will know what kind of man you are, for it shows me what your ideal of manhood is, and what kind of man you long to be.

—THOMAS CARLYLE

AS WE DELVE INTO OUR MASCULINITY, I WANT US TO BE OPEN AND honest in reevaluating our definitions of masculinity, to question where they come from. I also want us to be vulnerable by acknowledging that our masculinity has a dark side. It can inflict pain, and we will identify these socially accepted destructive behaviors and attitudes in ourselves and learn how to eliminate them. We will discuss how the flawed definition we have embraced has harmful effects on us.

When you hear the term *masculinity*, what comes to mind? Let's look at a few prototypical personas.

Ben is twenty-three years old and in his fifth year at a state university. He smokes too much weed and drinks heavily on the weekends. He loves watching sports and works out five days a week. He has trust issues because of betrayal by past girlfriends, and he has allowed his life to be defined by them, resulting in a loss of self-identity. He carefully manages his Tinder profile and is not looking for a serious relationship, and he is exploring his sexuality. He lacks self-discipline, is controlled by his feelings, and fears failure. Ben's life is controlled by fear, not courage, and he refuses to own his mistakes. He pleases people and doesn't know how to master himself. He's angry and refuses to acknowledge the childhood wounds from his father and others and has no idea what to do with his pain. He buries that trauma, thinking he put it to death. He talks to his mom daily and is protected from the harshness of life by his parents, so he has never had to grind out true virtues of selflessness, perseverance, sacrifice, and discipline for himself.

Cal is twenty-seven years old and still lives at home. He has unkempt facial hair, is obsessed with video games, and is a frequent consumer of pornography. He has a part-time job and lacks motivation to do anything. He procrastinates and allows his parents to take responsibility for him. Life is simple and easy living for Cal, free of financial and emotional pain. He has taken a few classes at a community college but is not sure what he wants to do in life. Cal is clueless about how to conquer himself. He doesn't know who he is or what he was made for, so he finds himself drifting. Depression is setting in, and he feels angry and lonely. He lacks self-control and self-confidence and doesn't build the grit and do the hard work to move forward. His mother still leads him, and his parents have protected him from the pain of life, creating a dependent little boy. He is arrested in his masculinity.

Chad lacks motivation to grow into manhood. He's even scared of manhood because it's confusing and means responsibilities. He feels inadequate. Chad was sexually abused at a young age, and he was physically and emotionally abused by his dad. His mother hovered, controlled, and dominated him, which has resulted in a sort of emotional marriage with his mother. His shame causes him to hide and pretend. His only emotion is uncontrolled anger, spilling out in rage. Chad is narcissistic and self-centered, thinking life must revolve around him. He doesn't know what to do with his pain, and suffering has no meaning to him. His key attribute is avoidance, refusing to enter his fear arena. He cashes in on the privileges of adulthood without ever paying the price of developing deep, lasting character for the treacherous journey ahead of him. He has plenty of masculinity, but it's in chaos. He misunderstands what it means, and his actions bring harm to himself and others. His maleness is unshaped and uncultivated, and his masculine impulses have become toxic. He operates as an adolescent boy. He doesn't know how to lead and master himself, lacks self-control in all areas, and masks his fears so he won't be discovered. He lacks self-awareness.

He doesn't understand that his attitude is like a cancer slowing destroying him from the inside—he remains unaware as it begins to cause extreme damage. He is a shadow of what he was created to be, and the implications are overwhelming if he doesn't get counseling.

Devin is forty-two and lonely. He has no authentic friendships and is clueless about how to raise his kids, so he tries to become their friend. He is angry and feels disrespected by his wife. She controls him and is disappointed in him—he can never get anything right. His sex life is zilch, he's overweight, and he medicates his pain with alcohol, drugs, porn, religion, and career achievement. He feels unfulfilled even though he has a lot of diversions. Devin realizes his life has no meaning, and he has no influence. He is depressed and, at times, anxious that his life hasn't turned out the way he thought it would. His prescriptive Christianity didn't work, and the wounds from his father are causing him to finally spiral downward. He can't keep it together anymore.

Edward is sixty-five and now on the downside. He is deeply dissatisfied that his career didn't give him the significance he longed for. He gave himself to his career, which ultimately defined his identity. He was intoxicated by its power and the self-image he believed would satisfy him. He provided the very best for his family, but what did it cost him? He deals with the pain by believing a lie. He sacrificed his wife and children on the altar of his ego. He is emotionally detached from his children, and he and his wife pretended that all was well until she finally divorced him. He wonders what legacy he is leaving outside of his wealth. He lives a sad, empty life, realizing he never fulfilled his purpose, the reason he came into this world.[1]

Can you relate to any of these personas? Did these scripts touch you, tag you, shame you, cause you to get sad or angry? Perhaps they articulated who you are and how you feel and left you hopeless and discouraged. My intent was to speak the current truth concerning the masculinity crisis all of us as males are experiencing in some way or another.

TOXIC MASCULINITY

I am aware that *toxic* is an explosive word and has been used to beat the hell out us. Whatever you do, don't check out; rather, hear me out! I think you will be able to relate more than you think.

You may have heard the phrase *toxic masculinity* used in media and popular culture, but what does it really mean? Toxic masculinity refers to the cultural pressures felt by many men to behave according to certain "manly" stereotypes, such as acting tough, avoiding emotions, and seeking to dominate those around them. These behaviors have been shown to be harmful to men's mental health and have serious consequences for society.

The *Journal of Clinical Psychology* defines *toxic masculinity* as "the constellation of socially regressive masculine traits that serve to foster domination, the devaluation of women, homophobia, and wanton violence."[2] If you've made it this far in the book, you know this kind of masculinity is the opposite of what we're aiming for.

Toxic masculinity harms every aspect of our lives. It creates isolation, depression, anxiety, suicide, a warped self-image, and loneliness. Toxic men often fail to seek medical help or counseling, and they mask their shame and self-hatred. They fear emotions and are stubbornly committed to being something they're not.

It can damage relationships through poor communication, emotional disengagement, and physical distance. Toxic men may not be alone, but they are lonely, and that can lead to betrayal, passivity, disingenuity, and arrogance. They have unresolved pain and anger and are mean, opaque, and unapproachable. They're inauthentic and refuse to be vulnerable. They're fearful, unfaithful, and prone to outbursts of anger, and they often medicate their pain through alcohol, drugs, porn, workaholism, exercise, and materialism.

It can also be harmful to society at large: toxic masculinity leads to rape culture, sexual harassment, violence, and abuse. It creates aggressive bullies and hypermacho, unemotional men. The toxic man always knows the answer and must be right. He is misogynistic, antifeminist, homophobic, and aggressive against any feminine qualities in other men.

If these descriptions packed a left-hook punch on point for knockdown and caused your legs to wobble, you're not alone. We don't want to admit it's that bad, so we simply deny, lie low, and judgmentally point our finger at other men. Each of us needs to take a tough and honest look at our own behaviors and get them right. We need to be committed to embracing one direction: forward. The choice to simply stand in the status quo is wrong and cowardly. Our masculinity should bring strength, courage, and hope to every relationship. Our power is to be used for good.

This aggressive and intolerant version of masculinity has shaped young men for generations. Terry Kupers, psychiatrist at the Wright Institute, describes toxic masculinity as "the standard upon which the 'real man' is defined . . . [founded in the] domination of women and a hierarchy of intermale dominance [and] is also shaped to a significant extent by the stigmatization of homosexuality and the maintenance of imbalanced power across gender roles in normative culture."[3]

Because of masculinity's stifling rules and roles, many men who don't fit the definition have been left in the margins, unable to be a "real man." A man's definition of masculinity shapes him and guides him. Sadly, the common masculine ideal is flawed, unattainable, and toxic, and it gives most men an unhealthy blueprint with which to shape their own identity. This blueprint shapes how these men relate to women, their family, and other men and how they find their place in the world.

Sadly, many men then adopt a false self, a masculine persona, denying and rejecting their true self through this mask to be accepted and to play the role stereotypical masculinity requires. Harris O'Malley, writing for the Good Men Project, states that "men are still taught that they have to be *tough* . . . and *part* of that toughness means—oddly enough—being overly concerned with how others *perceive* that toughness. After all, you wouldn't want the Gender Police to take away your man card for admitting to having your fee-fees hurt, would you?"[4]

"Clinging to this toxic form of masculinity is harmful to all of us."[5] It leads to feelings of "physical inadequacy, emotional inexpressiveness, subordination to women, intellectual inferiority, and performance failure."[6] Specifically, our masculine personalities depend on the ways we assign meaning to specific situations in our lives.[7] When a man defines himself by traditional masculine gender roles, he is potentially exposing himself to this kind of stress.

Progress is never a straight line, uninterrupted from A to B to C. It's always off-roading, interrupted, up and down, and curvy. Hidden in the status quo myth of conventional masculinity lies a plethora of disturbing consequences for men that we need to expose and reconcile.

When we've fully deconstructed and reconstructed our definition of masculinity, we will have cleansed ourselves of damaging attitudes, habits, and unattainable dysfunctional roles, after which we can become the best versions of ourselves and paint the right masculine picture for younger men to emulate. For example, how we view and relate with women will be drastically different. We will cease to view women as subordinate or inferior, and we will begin to actively support the push for equity.

GENDER ROLES

There are multiple defining voices of masculinity. These many voices are like dogs on leashes barking, pulling, and pointing in various directions. Evangelical and Catholic communities bark about strict gender roles and what it means to be a man or a woman. Some of the masculine qualities embraced by the church are positive, but others are toxic. The Armed Forces likewise adhere to distinct gender roles. Athletic teams, feminist organizations, women's groups, fraternities and sororities, large global companies, and political organizations all define masculinity in various ways. For the most part it's a free-for-all, and we end up choosing the community definition that fits us best. On the other hand, an evolution of gender roles that threatens traditional guidelines about what are acceptable and unacceptable behaviors is surfacing and taking form.

Gender roles are stereotypes in any given culture about how we're expected to act, speak, dress, and conduct ourselves based on our assigned sex. The same sorts of unreasonable social expectations placed on men are also placed on women. In Western culture, women were traditionally expected to be quiet, nurturing, passive, and weak. They were expected to dress in "feminine" attire and be interested in homemaking, raising children, and staying attractive for their husbands, rather than having any ambitions of their own. Even at the university level, you see some gender roles in the degrees men and women pursue or are encouraged to pursue, although this has changed dramatically in the last three decades.

Religious communities, family, media, peers, gangs, and cultural traditions all present their own versions of masculinity that influence gender roles and cultural definitions. We are exposed to these versions of manliness at an early age, and they have incredible impact on each of us, for better or for worse. Much of our understanding is simply handed down from families or the community, and these authorities may see everything as black and white, without taking time for critical analysis, changing culture, or the grayness of life. For example, the gender role of women doing all the cooking and cleaning is something that, sixty years ago, was much more widely accepted than it is today (and for good reason!). Today, when a guy wants to impress a woman, he invites her over to a meal he has prepared with ambiance! That would have been unheard of decades ago; it would have been deemed "girly." Gender roles are shifting, and that's good!

Here are some gender role questions you need to ask yourself:

- What gender roles do you play out and why?
- Who taught you those roles? Where did they come from and why?
- Why should you abandon some of these roles?
- What gender roles do you feel more comfortable with and naturally align with you?
- How have those roles harmed you and made you incomplete as a man?

- Why do some of these roles make you feel inadequate as a man?
- What gender roles do you like and why?

Thankfully, for the most part, I was raised differently. My aunt on my father's side was the first woman to attend college from the town of Nowata, Oklahoma, in the 1930s, and her sister followed, graduating from Oklahoma State University in the 1940s. My mother took some classes at Oklahoma State while working as the secretary for the president of OSU and putting my father through school. She was a first-generation college student in her family, even though she didn't graduate. My mother had a significant career outside the home, so, for me and my sisters, our family culture always elevated women and broke some of the stereotypical gender roles. I am proud of this heritage.

However, my family also stuck to many of those traditional roles. My dad had always mowed and taken care of the lawn—every man in the town had. They'd taken pride in that beautiful green lawn. It had been a man's job, and if you failed in this, your masculinity was in question. As you can discern, two concepts of what defines masculinity collided in what I learned from my family.

Like many men, I bought into some of these stereotypes for a long time. As a young married man, I had a skewed and misguided concept of what was acceptable and unacceptable in a married couple. One day, when I came home from work and pulled into my driveway, I found my wife mowing the lawn. I got out of the car and asked her with a snarky attitude, "Why are you mowing the lawn?" The second question that came out of my mouth revealed a lot about my fragile male self-image and fears: "What will the neighbors think about me?"

She looked at me dumbfounded and said, "John, I come from the farm. The women mow the lawn and paint the house because the men are in the fields all day. And besides that, I like mowing the lawn—it gives me some immediate gratification." Unspoken, but clear as day from her tone of voice, I heard her saying, *So get over it, buddy.*

When I drove up the drive the following day, my neighbor Lance was out in the yard and motioned for me to come over. I walked over, and he said, "John, how did you get your wife to mow the lawn?" I lost it! My neighbor was watching and evaluating! I told him the whole story, and we belly-laughed for fifteen minutes. When I pulled into the drive the following week, guess who was mowing Lance's lawn. Yup—Laurie, his wife!

Luckily, my father never viewed weeping as unmasculine. I never heard him say anything negative about it. I don't remember crying in front of him, and I only remember seeing him cry a few times, usually at a funeral. He showed who he was more through what he didn't say but simply allowed. His life modeled what he believed.

My parents were typical Oklahomans, and that meant sacrificing for family first. They did this superbly, with such grace. It was just the way it was. I laughed with them later in life, as my active lifestyle kept them very busy! They never complained. I believe one of my first aha moments of their virtue of sacrifice was in sports. My parents were always at my events, even every out-of-town wrestling match. They sometimes drove one or two hours to my high school matches. I assumed every parent did this, but I was soon rocked into reality that that was not true. I remember looking into the visitor stands and seeing just a small number of parents from my hometown of El Dorado, Kansas, and surmising that lots of my teammates' families did not make the trip. There were also more mothers than fathers in those stands. What was the norm for me was not for my teammates. My dad and mom both attended and supported me, whether it was wrestling, football, track, band concerts (I played the saxophone), musicals, or choir. Selflessness was their definition of love. Their demonstration of sacrifice served me well, and it became one of the character values I chose to embrace. I'm thankful that this value was imprinted on me by both my mom and my dad.

I was lucky: many men learn the wrong kind of masculinity from their families. But there is a better, healthier masculinity emerging on the horizon. We need to educate ourselves and passionately embrace it. We need to call out our brave to stand up for what is right against injustice, embracing our emotions and expressing them appropriately. We need to grow beyond the old form of masculinity and narrow gender roles.

BRAVEASS REFLECTION

- The old, fake masculinity is harmful, narrow, and out of touch. How has it affected you personally?
- Toxic masculinity is not just a label, it's a damaging, misguided mindset. What areas of your masculinity have been toxic?
- Make a bullet list of how you want your masculinity to manifest and why.

CHAPTER 8

TRUE MASCULINITY

> True masculine power happens when courage, integrity, vulnerability, compassion, awareness, and the capacity to take strong action are all functioning together.
>
> —ROBERT AUGUSTUS MASTERS,
> *TO BE A MAN: A GUIDE TO TRUE MASCULINE POWER*

I PROPOSE THE FOLLOWING BRAVEASS TRUTHS OF MASCULINITY. Masculinity involves the courage, strength, and boldness to be vulnerable, honest, self-controlled, and resilient; to take risks and accept responsibility; to be loving and selfless; and to humbly own our mistakes. Additionally, this personal courage, strength, and boldness would extend into a man's ability to take a stand against injustice, to speak truth, to affirm, and to build trusting relationships with others.

In her 2015 book *Rising Strong*, Brené Brown states, "To be vulnerable is to be brave." We unleash the power of our masculine through acts of bravery. The courage to live a vulnerable, honest, self-controlled, sacrificial, gritty, and bold life is authentic. And authenticity is attractive and brings honor to the masculine. There are certain elements that can help you embrace the new true masculinity, each leading to confidence and acceptance of who you really are.

PURPOSE

Our true masculinity is at its best when we know and live out our God-given purpose.

We all need to have purpose. We are adrift without it—never fulfilled, always searching. We have no sense of peace without direction. We must identify who we are, our calling, our strengths and abilities, and the character qualities we believe in. And then we must pursue those aspects of ourselves. Without them, we will live a directionless life that wanders toward negative self-image, discouragement, and sometimes addiction. The bottom line is that there is a reason you were created; you have a God-given design and purpose. There is freedom in the discipline of figuring out who we are, how we were designed, and then aligning our life with this reality. Doing so brings that sense of purpose, meaning, impact, and well-being—and, of course, confidence.

Without purpose, we will live an unfulfilled and haphazard life of discouragement and uselessness. Men without a purpose can find themselves in deep mental and emotional distress that can rule and destroy them. You must face your reality and raise your flag.

In college, I was keenly aware I was struggling to identify who I was and what my mission in life would be. I was clueless and felt frustrated that my future wasn't crystal clear, like it was for some of my fraternity brothers. Many of them knew without a doubt the direction they were headed. What was wrong with me? Why couldn't I make a decision and press on? These thoughts haunted me.

I excelled in pre-architecture, but it wasn't my passion, so I changed majors and went into science and business. But this too was unfulfilling. I was trapped by three years of financial and academic investment, so I decided to just finish the degree and cut my losses. I remember contemplating pursuing a master's degree right after my bachelor's, but luckily, I decided instead to enter the workforce for a few years and come back to the idea later. I did not want to make the same mistake again. I knew in my heart that I was still drifting, still in search of who I was.

The next six years of work experience changed everything. I joined a nonprofit organization and started coaching men in every area of their lives. This was the first time in my life I felt complete, fulfilled, and like I was doing something meaningful. I had never been this passionate about anything I had tried before in my quest for significance. I awoke from a deep sleep, like a bear coming out of hibernation. For the first time in my life, I found synergy; everything came together. I discovered who I was, what I was good at, and what my passions were—my purpose.

This job required me to help men think about who they were, but in order to be effective, I had to do the same. I needed to speak and mentor from experience. I learned things about myself that were helpful in my personal discovery journey. I did an exercise given to me by a mentor where I identified key moments in my life when I felt fulfilled, when I succeeded, and looked for a pattern. I also spoke with friends and colleagues, noting—mentally and emotionally—when others affirmed my leadership and design. I also received input on what they saw in my life through personal discussions and where I excelled. I listened to my heart about when I felt joy and fulfillment in what I was doing. My conclusion was that it didn't seem like a job; it was a passion. I have in turn used this exercise with other men on their journey in discovering how they were designed and the benefits they will contribute to society.

I was jazzed about my work, and I felt like I was making an impact in the lives of men. Eventually I sat down and did a reflection exercise, looking back over my life, and defined my purpose: I was created to coach, lead, counsel, empower, affirm, validate, heal, bless, and bring value to men. After being immersed in this fulfilling and powerful work for a decade, I had learned unbelievable lessons from the trenches. I decided to get a master's degree under the Educational Psychology department at the University of Nebraska–Lincoln in leadership and student development, with a thesis in mentoring. This decision continued to propel me toward my calling, and it has led to a meaningful career, adding purpose to my life.

We desperately need to identify who we are, why we were created, and then fulfill this destiny, influencing our relationships and our society. When we do this, we are at our best and offer our best.

HONESTY AND TRANSPARENCY

Our true masculinity is at its best when we are honest and transparent. The *Merriam-Webster Dictionary* states, "Honesty implies a refusal to lie, steal, or deceive in any way. Honor suggests an active or anxious regard for the standards of one's profession, calling, or position. Integrity implies trustworthiness and incorruptibility to a degree that one is incapable of being false to a trust, responsibility, or pledge."[1]

Honesty is the number one value we desire in our relationships. No relationship can grow or flourish without honesty. Trust is grounded in only one value—honesty. Being trustworthy and faithful puts to death a slew of issues that plague us personally as well as every other relationship we touch. Our dishonesty and unfaithfulness destroy and damage without discrimination. We must pursue faithfulness and trustworthiness in the decisions we make. It isn't a matter of knowing what is right; we know what's right—we just choose to deceive, usually for personal gain or sexual fantasies.

> "Honesty creates intimate connections and decreases the turbulence of life, while dishonesty always creates distance and problems that have to be dealt with in the future."
>
> —YUNG PUEBLO, INSTAGRAM POST

These decisions come from a place of selfishness and disregard, as well as disrespect to our commitment and promises to others and ourselves. We shine as men when we are trustworthy and faithful, and it brings us honor and respect.

We need to be open, honest, and transparent first with ourselves and then with other men. There comes a pinnacle moment in every man's life when he accepts his identity and stops the masquerade. This watershed is when he walks into accepting and being honest with his true self. The pretending takes lots of energy and the pleasing of others is draining because it's living a lie, or, at best, a half-truth. It makes you weary. When we accept ourselves with all of our mistakes and stop living for the acceptance and applause of others, we find the true self. The poser is put to death. When this happens, a new strength can finally emerge—a brave that was in you but had never been called out.

I was often at war with myself, feeling like I didn't measure up, striving to prove myself, and comparing myself with other men. It is a life of inner turmoil until you let go and simply accept, love, and respect yourself. We compare everything with each other. Our muscle, athleticism, smarts, appearance, abilities, finances, degrees, power positions, houses, and cars. That's the way we are; we constantly compare and then assess and give ourselves a score. We must let it all go and come to a defining moment to rule over our fear of the opinion of others, our opinion of ourselves, and the false definition of what it means to be male, and rather step onto that mat and wrestle. Your opponent may be your false self portraying something you are not because you are not yet secure with your true self.

We are at our best when we are transparent and honest with who we are and with our decisions. This is the place of strength, freedom, respect, and power.

GRIT TO ENDURE ADVERSITY

Our true masculinity is at its best when we have the will and grit to endure adversity. Without grit, you can't stick to your commitments. Angela Duckworth's work on grit measures the extent to which you approach life with it. Her research proves that grit trumps talent for succeeding. Gritty people overcome adversity and setbacks. They simply don't give up or give in; they persevere.[2] As Gary John Bishop said in his book *Unfu*k Yourself*, "When you're not sure if you're following the right path, when you've been knocked down a few times too many, it's completely fine to get discouraged—hell, even defeated. What's not ok is to stop." In wrestling, grit was when you got your butt kicked but you didn't quit. You showed up the next day. You pushed through the hunger that gnawed at you 24 hours a day and disciplined yourself to practice conquering this feeling during exhausting physical practice. "No matter the domain," says Duckworth, "the highly successful had a kind of ferocious determination that played out in two ways."[3] They were resilient, and they knew what they wanted. They had our first two key traits of the modern man: purpose and grit.

Our lives are full of adversity. We get one calamity taken care of, and along comes another; they are never-ending. No one ever told me life was going to be this hard; we just have to figure it out. Shakespeare once wrote, "Let me embrace thee, sour adversity, for wise men say it is the wisest course." We have a decision to make every time adversity comes along: choose to enter the fray, or run away.

I love what Ryan Holiday says: "Obstacles are a part of life. Things happen, stuff gets in our way, situations go awry." Once I accepted this truth, I was able to move forward, embracing the fact that obstacles will get in the way. It freed me and drastically changed my perspective. With acceptance, I was able to focus on six important questions:

- What can I learn from this situation?
- How could accepting this event change me for the better?
- What would it look like to process my hurt and pain in a healthy way?
- How do I choose to stand up and call out wrongdoings without being angry or vindictive?
- What would it look like to rise above others' mistreatment and refuse to treat them with the same ugliness?
- Why is anger appropriate when abuse has been inflicted on me?

There are no other choices. Sometimes I get a left hook that stuns me, and other times I throw a left hook. I am always learning and pivoting from my punches. Change will never happen on the sidelines; it happens in the fray, on the mat, wrestling with all your might. Confidence and conviction are forged through this process. When our fears subvert this process, we become weak and undependable, and we lack stability when we need courage and strength most. Dale Carnegie reminds us that "inaction breeds doubt and fear, [and] action breeds confidence and courage. If you want to conquer fear, do not sit at home and think about it. Go out and get busy." We are at our best when we have the will and the grit to endure adversity, to call out determination, perseverance, and an attitude of not giving up or giving in. Grit begets glory.

COURAGE

Our true masculinity is at its best when we are courageous.

Courage is the catalyst for all other virtues. Courage is the inner fortitude of the heart. I'm a gym guy and spend time training my body every week; that's outer fortitude. For me, my rule is that I spend the same amount of time forging inner fortitude. Whether it's outer or inner fortitude, building it requires discipline, consistency, perseverance, and a commitment to change. You also need deep self-respect and hope. When we develop courage, we become whole, bringing a oneness of spirit and soul. Our integrated self produces self-satisfaction, confidence, self-respect, hope, and joy. We like who we are and who we continue becoming. Courage is commanding our fears.

A decade ago, I had to reinvent myself. I had to identify and pursue a new purpose. Talk about a Mount Everest! The nonprofit I worked for, The Navigators, fired me after twenty-seven years, and I decided to not go back into the nonprofit world tied to Christianity. I had to figure out how to adjust my skill sets, passions, and calling outside of that culture. Luckily all my strengths were transferable; I just had to figure out how to use them within a new culture. My reinvention lasted for several years. It wasn't a quick fix but a constant recalibration along the journey. I figured out a new mission and calling, set goals, and started the pursuit, identifying actions for the path forward toward the ideal John. You never arrive; you just keep tweaking as you learn! But courage was crucial along the entire journey.

Holy moly has it taken a lot of trial and error, getting up and back into the ring and reclaiming John. It's like when I was a wrestler: What wrestler gets up and leaves the mat when another scores points on him? In a flash, you can also score points on him, and it completely changes the outcome because you stayed in the fight without giving up or giving in. And, yes, opponents may score lots of points, but you stay on the mat until the buzzer sounds. The recalibration demands perseverance, determination, and self-discipline, as well as an attitude of being a learner. Most of all, it demands courage. We are at our best when we call out the courage inside us to enter the arena and defeat whatever it is that wants to conquer us.

HUMILITY AND HEALING

Our true masculinity is at its best when we are humble. Men are at their best when they pursue wholeness and healing, which will demand humility. We hate admitting we need help. The fact is that your pain has control over what you do. The lie we believe is that needing help equates to weakness—we abhor the thought of being weak. We spend all our energy and lifetime trying to prove to ourselves and others that we don't have any pain or sadness or hurt. That's bullshit. In reality, we become weak when we refuse to acknowledge that we need strength from others for our well-being. It takes humility to ask for help, to learn something new, or to acknowledge a need. Having the vulnerability to admit our needs makes us strong. Humility and healing are inseparable.

Healing means remaking yourself into something better, not just returning to some old state. I had to humble myself to admit I needed help and that I wanted to get well. My healing has made me into someone better than who I originally was. I'm more whole than I was before the process. I now frequently stop my judgmental attitude. I am more patient with people's projections at me, I let things go, I'm more understanding and empathetic, I apologize, I'm at peace with knowing I can't control others, and I'm more open to others' viewpoints and philosophies. My faith is also totally different from before.

A man I coached decades ago lost his father to cancer when he was in ninth grade. It was devastating. He would recount those months his dad was on his death bed: his father's pain from the cancer and their conversations at his dad's side. He was in deep pain from the loss and the loneliness of not having a father. He desperately wanted a dad to share life with. Many of us helped fill that void. Then, fifteen years later, his mother committed the selfish act of suicide. That's an incredible amount of pain and anguish for a family to navigate. The pain this man endured in his beginning years of manhood was extremely intense; none of us would want it. But he rose above all of this and continued his fight. He was an involved husband and father. He was an authentic friend to many; he shared his pain with other men and brought encouragement and hope. His lived-out faith with God was his foundation of strength, but most crucial was that he sought healing by asking for help. Sadly, Randy died this year from cancer. We had sweet conversations and reminisced about a lot of memories together before he passed.

We are at our best when we pursue wholeness and healing. Healing has direct effects on our significant relationships and on our society at large. We make the world a better place when we choose humility.

A LEGACY

Our true masculinity is at its best when we leave a legacy. We deeply desire to have impact because it proves that our life counts, that it has meaning. Our purpose resonates inside of us every time our masculinity influences another. We leave a legacy with our children, other men, women, family, friends, and society as a whole. Without knowing we've made an impact on those we care about, we feel hollow, and our self-worth is shattered.

I am often the first man other men share their pain with. Every time I invest in someone and I see transformational change, I tear up with pride. I know my life counts and has an impact. When another man opens his heart and asks for help, we make a sacred pact. Feeling like I've made an important change to someone's life is fulfilling; I know my purpose.

Part of my calling is to heal other men, to bring value and respect, to accept them, and to be a safe place for them to be vulnerable without judgment. I walk alongside them during a trial, validate and listen, and speak truth into their darkness.

Selflessness is at the heart of making an impact: servanthood, stewardship, sacrifice, thinking of others' interests above our own. When we embrace these virtues, our reason for living transcends ourselves. When we can grasp the impact that living for something bigger than ourselves can offer, we realize that our lives are not just about us. Instead, it's about choosing to use our lives to inspire or help others. After all, we're not going to be around forever, so we should become a part of something that will carry on.

One is too small a number for true impact and significant influence—these results come from being connected and collaborating with others. This teamwork creates synergy through

> "As much as we try to avoid thinking about it, our time on earth is limited. When you're gone, how will people remember you? At your funeral, people shouldn't have to guess about the kind of life you led or the legacy you left behind—what you stood for should be obvious from your actions in life."
>
> —DAVE SCHOENBECK, "JOHN MAXWELL'S LEADERSHIP LAW #21: THE LAW OF THE LEGACY"

the group's individual gifts, callings, skills, and personalities in concert. I have been involved in teams where this sweet spot is unleashed; we each valued and respected each other's contribution, supported one another, and allowed each other to lead the team at different times. We were in it together, and knew we needed each other. Meaning matters for a fulfilling and happy life. Our lives are happy and complete when we know we matter, and we know we are making the world better.

We create a space of trust with our honesty that allows our masculine power and energy to pass into a younger man, helping him in his masculine formation. As Richard Rohr says in his book *From Wild Man to Wise Man*, "We all need someone with inner authority who can let us know we are OK, that what we are going through is normal, and what battles are worth fighting. Sometimes we just need to hear from someone who believes in us, but who believes enough also to challenge us. Strangely, in their presence, the assurance and self-confidence are there, almost by magic, and almost embarrassingly so." We need other men—period.

We are at our best when we give our life away through mentoring the next generation of men, leaving our mark.

RESPONSIBILITY

Our true masculinity is at its best when we take responsibility. Being responsible is being trusted to do what we were asked to do, to live out the values we say are important to us, to be a man of our word, and to fulfill our promises, regardless of the cost. Responsibility needs accountability. Without accountability, we falter in being responsible. A lack of personal accountability in our current culture is destructive in every facet. It erodes respect and trust. When we refuse to take personal ownership and rectify our mistakes, society at large disrespects us—and rightly so. Society brands us as self-centered, self-absorbed liars; the word they use is *toxic*. It's a bad narrative, but until we own our own behavior, we will be disrespected and irrelevant as a gender. Only our actions will change the narrative. Taking personal accountability fosters positive change. It requires responding to our own mistakes and shortcomings with moral integrity.

It begins with showing up, willing to clean up our part, and choosing to make amends. It means we must say we're sorry and demonstrate sorrow through changed actions. That requires honesty, humility, and a secure self-image.

Our mistakes, our feelings, our words, our anger, our decisions, our leadership, our finances, our emotions, our mental health, our diet, our personal growth, our thoughts, our schedule, our gym time, our love life, our transgressions, our family, our fears—these are all our responsibility. Taking ownership will involve dealing with the consequences, which, many times, are intensely painful.

We must call out our brave and own up. This is where virtue is forged, by choosing responsibility. Taking personal ownership involves being accountable for your actions and life. People do what you inspect, not what you expect, and what gets measured gets better. That's the picture of accountability.

When others see this masculine trait, they realize they can trust you. Others want to be your friend and teammate because they can trust that you will do the right thing. We are at our best when others can trust us because we were devoted to being responsible.

SOCIAL JUSTICE

Our true masculinity is at its best when we stand up against what is wrong. We are responsible and should be held accountable for our God-given masculine power in response to social injustices. Instead of it being used for evil, divisiveness, bigotry, prejudice, and selfishness, our masculine power should be used for good, to put an end to injustice, and to find ways to better humanity. An aspect of toxic masculinity is when we ignore this calling and refuse the courage to enter public discourse against injustice. Sadly, many of us are on the wrong side of justice, especially if we are of the dominant race.

> "Injustice anywhere is a threat to justice everywhere."
> —MARTIN LUTHER KING, JR.

An example of true masculinity is William Wilberforce, a British politician and philanthropist who used his power to help lead the movement to abolish the slave trade. Another good example is Frederick Douglass, known for his work as an abolitionist and who was a supporter of the women's suffrage movement. He wrote, "All that distinguishes man as an intelligent and accountable being is equally true of women."[4] Other men using their masculine power for women's suffrage include George Francis Train, Thetus W. Sims, James Mott, Daniel Read Anthony, Henry Blackwell, and Francis Minor.

In 1927, William Danforth, founder of the Purina company, and his wife, Adda Bush, subsidized the construction of the Danforth chapel program through their Danforth Foundation, building twenty-two chapels, fifteen of which were on college campuses emphasizing the Christian faith. At Kansas State University, I used the Danforth chapel numerous times. Every chapel has a plaque that reads, "Dedicated to the worship of God with the prayer that here in the communion with the highest, those who enter may acquire the spiritual power to aspire nobly, adventure daringly, serve humbly." The Danforth Foundation also focused on national education scholarships for college students and in 2011 gave $70 million to the Donald Danforth Plant Science Center, where researchers focus on solving world hunger.

Two of the top foundations committed to the eradication of HIV are the Elton John AIDS Foundation and the Bill and Melinda Gates Foundation. Scottish American businessman and philanthropist Andrew Carnegie funded the construction of 2,509 Carnegie libraries between 1883 and 1929. In 2010, Bill and Melinda Gates (worth $88.5 billion) and Warren

Buffet (worth $74.2 billion) started The Giving Pledge, a campaign that encourages extremely wealthy people to give away half of their wealth to causes such as the alleviation of poverty, refugee aid, disaster relief, and global health. As of August 2020, the pledge has 210 signatories from twenty-three countries, totaling $1.2 trillion in wealth promised for worthy causes.

There is a legacy of men who used their masculine power to do good and better humanity. We are called to do our part in our communities. Whether it's supporting nondiscriminatory housing projects for the LGBTQ+ community, advocating for women leading in our churches, eliminating bigotry against people of color, standing against antisemitism, building playgrounds in our schools and communities, being involved in the Big Brother program, or protecting victims of abuse or child trafficking, we must empower our masculinity for the betterment of humanity. This is a picture of true masculinity: making a difference, standing against bigotry, and aligning ourselves with the marginalized, giving them dignity and creating hope for their future.

When we take a stand, other men will disagree and even fight against us. This has been the case throughout history, and it will never change.

We have a calling to stand on the right side—against hate, against devaluing the marginalized, and against bigotry—and to be generous with those in need. That's moral courage in action.

We are at our best as men when we make moral decisions to stand up against injustice.

"The strictest law sometimes becomes the severest injustice."

—BENJAMIN FRANKLIN

CHARACTER

Our true masculinity is at its best when we live out moral character. We often talk about character and its value, but few live it. We supposedly believe in virtue, but our lives speak the opposite. The bottom line is that character is taught and learned by example. But it's hard to live out because it has a price tag.

> "Is it ethical, legal, and moral? Ethical—does it follow the rules? Legal—does it follow the law? And moral—does it follow what you know to be right?"
>
> —ADMIRAL WILLIAM H. MCRAVEN,
> *THE WISDOM OF THE BULLFROG*

Character is only forged in the selfless, tough decisions that we are constantly faced with. Choosing to be honest, to do what's right, and to not compromise are often painful and can be costly.

Have you ever thought that your well-being is intertwined with the way you live your character? If you are constantly lying, living secrets, compromising, hating, holding grudges, or choosing to be vindictive and self-centered, you are not free emotionally. You are captive to negative and degrading attitudes that poison your soul and create incredible anxiety. Behind this curtain, you don't like who you are, you know your decisions are wrong, and you lack self-respect. It's a degrading place that zaps your energy and your self-worth. It's depressing and lonely. I know, I've been there.

Character is about doing what you say you will, sticking to your convictions. You earn respect for the choices and decisions you make to do what is right. As Carl Jung said, "You are what you do, not what you say you'll do." All relationships—business, spiritual, and personal—are based on trust. Living this kind of life makes you trustworthy. Without trust, every relationship falters, including leadership. Don't be deceived: regardless of how competent and skillful you are in your career, if you fail in character, you fail as a leader, and the consequences are grave.

Men are at their best when they make decisions based on character, on knowing right from wrong. This crucial piece of the new masculinity is visible to all who observe and follow. Our masculinity has undeniable power; it touches every relationship we encounter. People should walk away from our masculinity with hope, encouragement, courage, and resolve because of our integrity. Living out integrity brings honor to masculinity.

The revolution will produce men who know and live out the true meaning of what it is to be a man. I want to remind you of the following ten truths covered in this chapter; they are there to give you clarity and give you a true masculine guideline to follow!

- We are at our best when we identify who we are, why we were created, and then fulfill this destiny, influencing our relationships and our society.
- We are at our best when we take responsibility to lead, master, and conquer ourselves.
- We are at our best when we take off the false persona and accept who we really are.
- We are at our best when we have the will and the grit to endure adversity, to call out determination, perseverance, commitment, courage, and an attitude of not giving up or giving in.
- We are at our best when we pursue wholeness and healing. When we heal, our healing has direct effects on our significant relationships and on our society at large. We make the world a better place.
- We are at our best when we live from our integrity, when character matters.
- We are at our best when we bring value, encouragement, validation, and empowerment to other men and in other relationships; our blessing heals and brings power.
- We are at our best when we give ourselves to something bigger than ourselves.
- We are at our best when we take responsibility for and ownership of our mistakes. This kind of raw honesty,

vulnerability, and humility causes others to trust us and respect us as men.

- We are at our best when we stand against injustice, when we take responsibility and stand with the marginalized, the hated, and the mistreated, using our power to bring justice for everyone.
- We are at our best when we bring a gritty toughness that overcomes softness, weakness, helplessness, and fear. We rise above the situation and bring strength to all we touch. We become heroic.

I challenge you to join this revolution: choose to grapple by selecting to bring your masculinity to its best, grinding out these truths!

BRAVEASS REFLECTION

- What qualities of true masculinity are you currently living out?
- Which true masculinity quality do you need to focus on and why?
- When are you at your best as a man?

CHAPTER 9

USING YOUR MASCULINE POWER FOR GOOD

> Each time a man stands up for an ideal, or acts to improve the lot of others, or strikes out against injustice, he sends forth a tiny ripple of hope, and crossing each other from a million different centers of energy and daring, those ripples build a current that can sweep down the mightiest walls of oppression and resistance.
> —ROBERT F. KENNEDY, "DAY OF AFFIRMATION ADDRESS,"
> UNIVERSITY OF CAPE TOWN, 1966

IF YOU ARE A BOSS OR CEO, USING MASCULINE POWER FOR GOOD means making sure salary and job responsibility are based not on gender but on ability and credentials. This will require you to enter a fear arena because standing up for equality will always be met with resistance from other men who want to retain their power and privilege. They fear any change in the status quo that could upset the power imbalance.

Recently, I entered a career environment where a "good ole boys" club had dominated the scene for over forty years. After some time, I was keenly aware I had not been accepted into the club. I was constantly relegated to the sideline and never included in the decision-making. These men, at one time, had powerful voices, but because of cultural changes, they had become out of touch with the current reality and were a detriment to the company's future. But they refused to give up their sacred position, hiding behind decades-old successes. They were threatened by my reputation, experience, and current success. I was more qualified, had more experience and skills, and yet was refused a seat at the table. I was rejected and marginalized because I wasn't in the right group. I understood to some small degree what women and people of color must feel all the time.

A young woman eventually took the top job as director, and these men asked for a meeting with her. Without looping her in, a couple of the men asked me what I thought of her as the director. I knew this was a crucial point for her and for me. I chose to exalt her and her career path and what it brought to the table. I told them we were lucky to have such a competent and experienced director to lead us. I was able to affirm her in front of these men, using my masculine power for good and for equity.

Sadly, instead of using our masculine privilege for the betterment of others and for upholding the rights of the marginalized, many men have used their white masculine power position for their own personal gain and the injustice of others, protecting their power with undue influence. These toxic men have caused unbelievable harm. There's a reason it's called *toxic*; this behavior is poisonous and destructive.

As I have evolved in my masculinity, every area of my life has changed. How I view and accept myself, how I relate with other men, how I coach and mentor, how I engage with social justice issues, how I lead, how I act as a husband, and how I relate with women have all shifted toward positive support and empowerment. I became very justice-oriented, wanting to use my masculine power for good. I became a better listener, and from that I was able to understand the issues women face and not view them only through the lens of a privileged white male. Once I was able to do that, it helped me come to grips with their plight and my privilege.

I teach a cycling and bootcamp class for Group-X, and I was recently at a team meeting where the owner of the gym let us know he'd made the decision that no Group-X instructor could teach a class at another gym. A noncompete clause is common for personal trainers, but not for Group-X instructors. Most of these instructors are women. As I sat in this meeting—led by the owner, a man who also owned car lots and had only recently gone into buying gyms as a new profession—with fifteen women and only one other man in the room, I was at the crossroad of stepping into my fear arena. Would I use my male voice of power to speak up for these women, or would I remain silent? What would it cost me if I stood by the women? Would I be ostracized from the "male club" as a traitor? Would I eventually be removed for some ludicrous reason? These are valid questions you must ask yourself when determining whether you have the resolve to speak up.

I first had to control my anger. After listening to the women confront the owner with how unfair this decision was and how none of them could make a livable wage teaching classes at only one gym, and after listening to his uneducated, belligerent reasons for the decision, it was my turn to enter the fray. I stood and said I had worked at gyms in several states around the country, and no gym had this clause for Group-X instructors because no gym could employ them forty hours a week like they can personal trainers. I said that some of these women were single moms eking out a living and that this would throw them into poverty. I said we should be doing all we can as a gym to support these women, helping them in their profession, not exploiting them. These women increase the membership at the gym because of their talent, skill, degrees, and relational connections with everyone who participates in their classes. Sadly, the owner was belligerent and had to be right. He did not back down or change the policy.

After some heated debate, many women came up to me to express their gratitude for standing up against another man in their defense. I was proud of this moment, using my masculinity to stand against injustice for these women. Integrity is when your words and actions are aligned. It was puzzling to me that the new gym owner had several children, some girls, and that he would maintain such an exploitative position. What would he say in fifteen years if one of his daughters were in that room as a single mom with two kids?

I used to have the mindset that I was the sole protector for the women in my life, starting with my wife and daughter. I still believe it is a part of true masculinity, to protect and to save, but what I came to realize was women also protect and save. Women constantly sacrifice for their children, husbands, and humanity, even giving up their lives. Countless men who come from single-parent homes, where the mom gave up everything for her children, have a deep admiration, respect, and love for their mom.

Recently, I asked a group of men in a fraternity what it means to be masculine. Someone said it meant being the savior, protector, and provider. I challenged this thought by saying lots of women have given up everything to provide and protect their children. I believe it helped this group of men to rethink masculinity. As men I do believe we find meaning in protecting and providing, and this should be a hallmark of who we are.

I could totally relate to these young men in their thinking. They felt a calling to stand up for their future wives, significant others, and children, to be that provider who meets all their physical, emotional, and financial needs. There is something inside that wells up at that challenge. You see it as a priority. You will fight anyone who hurts her. You relish this position, and it touches a part of your soul nothing else can touch—the deeply masculine and vulnerable part of you, the courageous part of you, that strength. Everything else pales in comparison.

I believe men and women both have a God-given desire to protect and provide. In conversations with numerous women, they have also expressed a desire for a man to put them first, to be their hero. It creates safety, stability, and security. This is one way that men show their love, through their strength. Many men tend to take more risks in the protection, and many women respect, desire, and long for a man to do this for them.

I have often been amazed at the men in a fraternity who will stand with a woman who has been raped, harassed, or assaulted. They have taken a stand against another male—a fraternity brother—to side with the woman. In this moment, they are protecting her by standing with her, believing her, and honoring her. They use their masculinity to empower her feminine power. Despite the bad narrative the media has portrayed of all fraternities (some of which is completely true), I have seen numerous men stand with these women. It is such a beautiful picture every time that makes me proud of these men. Men need to join the revolution using their masculine power for good—to support and empower rather than oppress and assault. This should be the default for all men, not just an ideal.

USING YOUR MASCULINE POWER FOR GOOD

BRAVEASS REFLECTION

- Society and the "good ole boy" system give men power at the expense of women and people of color. What will you do if you see this happen?

- Using your masculine power for good means standing up against those old systems and tearing them down. How do you use your masculine power for good?

- We all have an innate call to protect the people we love, and women are powerful protectors as well. What is the interplay between men protecting women and women protecting men?

CHAPTER 10

THE IMPORTANCE OF MALE FRIENDSHIPS

> A friend is one that knows you as you are, understands where you have been, accepts what you have become, and still gently allows you to grow.
>
> —UNKNOWN

I THINK ABOUT ECCLESIASTES 4:9–12 AND REMEMBER THAT WE WERE not created to be alone. We need one another. Two are always better than one. If you fall, your friend can join you and help you, but if you're alone, then you are overcome. We thrive when we have authentic and candid relationships. We need other men with whom we can be honest, without being judged or condemned—men who will listen and get into the arena with us. We need male friends, which are completely different from female friends.

One center dedicated to trauma treatment for young men says that "strong male friendships in adolescence are correlated with extremely positive health benefits."[1] One research study in 2016 found that strong male friendships help to release oxytocin in the brain, which can increase resilience in difficult situations and can lower stress levels.[2] Another study in 2017 found that male-to-male friendships, or "bromances," can actually be more emotionally satisfying than romantic relationships and can provide a better outlet for emotional support.[3]

We need sacred male friends we can be vulnerable with and trust with our secrets. We need a few men who are set apart from other men with whom we can be completely transparent, without judgment. Not everyone falls into this category. You must wisely choose who you will be vulnerable with. These sacred friends are set apart from the rest of our friends. They will keep your confidence, accept you just the way you are, listen and not try to fix you, give you time and space for pain and suffering, encourage you, speak truth to your lies, be patient with you, and kick your ass when needed. I'm grateful for Derli, Steve, Chris, Bill, Dave, Mike, Gabe, Jason, Zach, and Ron. They were (and still are) who I needed when I came out as a gay man. "Men have been programmed to believe that they are not allowed to be vulnerable, show emotions, or allow people to get too close to them. This forces them to lead a lonely life," states Sean Galla, a facilitator for male friends' groups.[4] These men have allowed me to be vulnerable without judgment. I trust them. I'm better because of them; they have been instrumental in my healing.

There is something about my accepting and vulnerable personality that often leads men to share their deepest pain with me, and for many, it's the first time they have ever shared it. In that moment of trust, they break through their fear and enter their private fear arena. This is the beginning of their healing process. It's one of the most beautiful moments in relationships. I am able to bless another man with masculine affirmation and acceptance, which is completely different from a female affirmation.

In one such experience, a guy shared with me how he was molested at an early age by a neighbor boy and how his brother watched and didn't stop it. As he shared it, he started weeping. He had a stocking cap on and continued to pull it down over his eyes. It resembled shame and not wanting to be seen, but to hide. I later gave him a book on sexual abuse. He brought a brown paper bag to put it in, not wanting anyone to know what he was reading because of how they would label him with his trauma. Our conversation was sacred. He courageously entered the road less traveled to healing and hope. I accepted him, listened to him, loved him, and affirmed that it wasn't his fault. We need trusting male relationships to share vulnerably. All vulnerability takes courage, and this man called out his brave. You can have no intimacy, connection, belonging, or love without allowing yourself to be seen. Transparency is letting others set their eyes on who you truly are.

In my friendships, we get involved with each other in life's challenges and adversities. We provide counsel and guidance, as well as needed support during stressful times and for major decisions. These friendships have helped me explore alternative perspectives and are a part of my mental and emotional wellness.

I have found in my own life that shame leads to self-hate, and self-hate leads to self-destruction. I was in this cycle for years. Author Brennan Manning said to me over lunch one day, "John, God loves you just the way you are, not the way you should be." My aha moment from Psalms 139 was that God doesn't hate or reject what He created; other people might, but God doesn't. And God understands you. He has seen everything you have ever done and still accepts and loves you. God loves us with a steadfast, everlasting, unchanging love, regardless of what we have done or how we were created. This was a pivotal moment in accepting that I was born gay. I remember saying to a former friend, "You abandoned me, but you need to know God never abandoned me."

No one can walk out of their secrets alone. We try and try to fix our issues by ourselves, but we never can, and it always takes us down. It's too confusing. Many people spend a lifetime with their secrets, causing themselves and those they love devastating and permanent injury. We believe the lie that our issues will not affect others, but they will. Hurt people hurt people. Unhealthy people have an impact on all people in their sphere of influence.

Being vulnerable with sacred male friends is the way out of that fear. Being vulnerable allows ourselves to be completely visible. You may ask, *Why does it need to be with another man?* Well, would you want another man sharing deep, intimate issues with your wife over coffee or a Busch Light every week? Sure, women have insights. My counselor, Kristine, is one, but she is a professional. And men get men. We understand each other because we are the same gender. Yes, insights from women are phenomenal, and we need them too!

> "When young men ignore the need for male friends, it often leads to a generation of emotionally stoic, autonomous, and isolated adult males with personal issues. These men try to live up to societal expectations and beliefs of what a man is and what a male friendship should look like."
>
> —SEAN GALLA, "MALE FRIENDS: THE IMPORTANCE OF MAKING MALE FRIENDS," MENSGROUP.COM

We need to develop a clan of trusting male friends for a lifetime or for different phases in our lives. During the phase in my life when I had children, I met weekly with two other men for lunch, and we would share what was going on with our kids and give each other advice. Among the three of us, we had eleven kids, at every age level. We bonded as men because of our kids, which led to lots of other discussions concerning our own life issues and our marriages.

Many times, we shy away from deeper male relationships because we are competitive with each other and we don't want to admit that we are not perfect. It makes us feel needy and weak, and we hate that. We struggle to trust. It's hard for us to trust another man with our secrets, especially if we have been betrayed before. We don't want to hand over power to other men with our vulnerability because they could use it against us. Our egos rule us, and we lack control over it. But the risk is worth it. Bottom line: I'm now only vulnerable with those who have earned the right. I'm very selective.

It starts with choosing a guy from your work group, the gym, happy hour, church, your softball team, or your kids' sport practices and games. For example, just recently, I was in a work group of men at Kansas State University, and from that, a couple of us have started having lunch together and sharing about our lives. As time has progressed, we are sharing more vulnerably. It feels organic and natural. If you're not around men often, then take the risk and join something—a club or a sports league, like bowling, volleyball, or softball.

I've been in lots of men's groups ranging from just two of us to several, which have had incredible impact in sharpening me. We met weekly, set boundaries and expectations, kept everything confidential, made commitments to each other,

"Vulnerability is based on mutuality and requires boundaries and trust. It's not oversharing, it's not purging, it's not indiscriminate disclosure, and it's not celebrity-style social media information dumps. Vulnerability is about sharing our feelings and our experiences with people who have earned the right to hear them. Being vulnerable and open is mutual and an integral part of the trust-building process."

—BRENÉ BROWN, *DARING GREATLY*

listened, and affirmed and shared about our private pain, professional issues, our marriages, and our kids.

And I am indebted to them for making me better. There is a peace and freedom to be known without judgment, to be accepted and not have to perform, and to be genuinely loved and cared for. We are lonely. We desire the depth of a bonding relationship with other men, but we are afraid to open up and be real with who we are, and that stops us from connecting and keeps us lonely.

There is freedom and connection when we open up with each other. We come to realize lots of us deal with the same shit, have the same baggage. We suddenly recognize that we are not alone. And that's a good place to be with other men. To many, men are alone in their fight. Once again, it will take courage to be honest with other men, but it is the foundational key, and without being brave, it will not happen.

An ideal male friendship is based on mutual respect, trust, shared confidentiality, laughter and making fun of each other, vulnerability, affirmation, nonjudgmental connection, and authenticity. True friends protect us, serve as our alternative conscience, and can be our salvation. When you take the mask off, connection happens. But you must initiate it: get out of the house and join other men in a hiking club, a book group, yoga, a barbeque, gardening, art, a weekly Japanese Go game, biking, whiskey or craft beer tasting, or helping each other with things around your homes. You need to get around other men and then pair off.

For example, a neighbor of mine, some other guy friends,

and I poured a concrete slab for my garage. We worked together, completed the goal, and then we had dinner together. We bonded. Another time, I needed to drywall my basement but was clueless about how to do it. Lonnie, a friend who knew how to drywall, came over to help, and we did it together. As we worked, we talked about life, and our connection deepened.

"The first step to breaking down the emotional walls and forming a meaningful connection is understanding that true masculinity is based on being emotionally grounded," says Jack Davis, founder of Uncivilized Man. "This means that you must learn to accept the feelings that come into your life, reason with them, and understand that all men go through a spectrum of personal emotions. Sharing those personal emotions with a close friend takes strength, courage, and the ability to build a bridge for their emotions as well. Being empathetic to other men can allow you to make male friendships that have more meaning and depth."[5]

Male friendships traditionally revolve around a common purpose or mission to accomplish. We are better at getting to know each other first as we participate in an activity or mission together. We become friends as we work together or join to accomplish something. So that can be your first step: find a mission. For eight years, I have taken men to Nicaragua to bring clean water to villages where the water is contaminated. Contaminated water causes dysentery, and because of this the death rate of children under the age of five is high. I had dysentery while I was living in Zambia, and it knocked me flat for weeks. I lost over twenty-five pounds. We bust our butts digging four-foot trenches in extreme heat. At noon, we only get two peanut butter and jelly sandwiches. We work side by side with the people in the village. In the evening after dinner, we review our day and what we learned. Through this experience, we bond as men. Oh yeah, and the coldest beer on the planet is in Nicaragua!

Next, trust is paramount in male relationships. It's trusting and relying on the character quality of confidentiality, honesty, and integrity. These qualities allow us to be dependent and transparent. Trust needs to be established before we can open up to each other. Building trust will involve degrees of opening up that build upon each other.

You may develop what I call *drunk language.* It's fun going to happy hour or watching sports together and throwing down some brewskies. Our inhibitions come down when we drink with each other, and our language changes. Many times, we share emotionally during these times. We share hurts from women, other men, and relationships.

I see this all the time with university men in the fraternities, as well as in the residence halls. When they drink with each other, their language changes and they share deeper issues. Listening, accepting, mutually identifying with pain, and sharing are all healing. Sometimes they will cry with each other as each one opens up with their pain. It doesn't happen repeatedly, but when it happens, they bond, they enter a different level of friendship.

Commonalities also naturally bring us together, like the

gym, sports, clubs, kids, religion, cars, music, careers, and divorce. We share through our commonalities. We can talk about our divorce and its hurts, the music we enjoy and why, or our careers and how their ever-evolving dynamics affect us.

Vulnerability is crucial for male friendships. It can be tough for us because it makes us feel weak, and we hate feeling weak. But allowing each of us to be fully seen is the catalyst for deep connection. When we are brave enough to be vulnerable, we can establish respect, acceptance, and value, and these are bonding qualities. They bring a sense of belonging.

Finally, we need shared respect and honor. We will gravitate toward other men we respect because of their behavior and decisions. We want to get to know them. We honor them by wanting to be like them. They matter. We want to be with other men who call us to be our best selves. Respect and honor allow us to depend on each other; they fuel the truth that our life and their life matters, and together we both become better.

In many ways, we are influenced and shaped by who is around us. There's a proverb that states, "Tell me who your friends are, and I will tell you who you are." Which men I choose to allow in my inner friendship circle is extremely important because they have the power to either sharpen me or make me dull. One truth I learned in college is from Proverbs 27:17: "Iron sharpens iron as one man sharpens another." I need wise and humble men who are lifetime learners I respect, where we are committed to making each other better husbands, fathers, leaders, friends, and contributors to society. I need men who can protect me from my shortcomings, which will derail and dishonor me. Additionally, when I do blow it, I need to know that they will not abandon me or reject me in my hour of need, that they will stay with me, help heal my wounds, and call me to resilience and strength. I need to know that they will unconditionally love me in the middle of my train wrecks.

NOT ALONE BUT LONELY

In her article "All the Lonely Men: American Men Are Facing a Silent Epidemic: Their Loneliness," Sonora Jha explains that loneliness poses significant challenges to nearly 61 percent of Americans, which can increase the risk of premature death. The detrimental effects of loneliness on health can be equated to smoking fifteen cigarettes per day. Men struggle with reaching out for help due to society's masculine expectations that frown upon vulnerability, which is reinforced by homophobia. Fear of being labeled as "gay" often prevents straight men from seeking friendship or asking for support.[6]

During a very lonely time in my life, in my early fifties, I spent five Christmases alone at the same hotel in Denver. I'd have a great meal, go to a movie, watch TV, and spend some time reading and journaling. Talk about lonely. I could have been with my sisters' families, but I decided to just be alone. It was a rough stretch in my life. I learned invaluable lessons through this loneliness. One lesson taught me to be content with being alone and not needing others all the time. There is strength in being at peace in the middle of loneliness. After my divorce, I was alone. I was lonely, but I was free. Before my divorce, I wasn't alone. I was already lonely, and I was trapped.

I often think about how lonely my father was. He had no friends that he shared his life with. I never saw another man visit him, and I never saw him meet with any other men. The exception was the men he played golf with during the summer. But playing golf with these men never translated into connections outside of golf. He was incredibly lonely, with no one to share his struggles with or get counsel from or have fun with. Looking back on my marriage, I was not alone, but I was incredibly lonely. This is true for many men.

Yet one area of deep pain I have experienced is being abandoned and rejected by men who were my best friends. In the midst of my biggest mistake, when I committed infidelity and acknowledged I was gay, they left me—more for who I was than for what I'd done. Friendship has a cost, and the cost was too high for them.

Abandonment is a tough place. I have grieved over this, learned valuable lessons from it, and have come to a place of peace. I have learned how to carry it. A true friend never leaves you in your darkest hour. They join your fight, willing to share your fate. The fight is the discouragement from a relational loss—a wife who leaves you, children who have limited their connection with you, a dramatic change in your financial situation, a drop into depression and discouragement, a decision to leave your religious community, or regret about a poor decision.

We all desire to be loved in the face of our brokenness. A true friend accepts us despite our tragedies and mistakes. As I state earlier, during this time, I did have a few friends who stuck with me, never left, grieved with me, listened to my pain, spoke truth to me, and walked with me on the long road to my recovery. And I made new friends who took the place of the ones who left. They gave me the true picture of friendship, hope, respect, and meaning because they loved me.

Brené Brown comments in *Braving the Wilderness: The Quest for Belonging and the Courage to Stand Alone*, "True belonging doesn't require us to change who we are; it requires us to be who we are." We need to accept each other for who we truly are. One of our basic needs, according to Pavlov, is belonging. To belong means you're accepted, you're worth connecting with, and you matter. That's the basis of true friendship that passes the test of time.

We thrive when we have authentic, vulnerable, honest, and confidential relationships. That's where true connection and deep, meaningful relationships are formed. Without this, we become lonely, and that is not a healthy place to live.

We need to build authentic male relationships where we belong, where we matter, and where we are worth connecting with.

A good friend is someone who chooses

- to be courageous by being honest, transparent, and vulnerable with a few selected men;
- to be accepting, regardless;

- to be humble;
- to be a listener and a learner;
- to not fix but just value the conversation;
- to get permission to say something that might be painful;
- to seek to understand and not judge;
- to be comfortable when he doesn't agree with a conviction you hold close;
- to personally sacrifice, saying no to themselves and yes to your needs;
- to never discard you based on an ideology; and
- to value the relationship over being right.

BRAVEASS REFLECTION

- We need sacred male friendships. Who will you ask to join you in a deeper friendship? Who will you choose to be honest and vulnerable with?
- Strong male friends keep us emotionally and mentally healthy. Journal on how this statement is true and choose who you will continue to go deeper with and why.

CHAPTER 11

ARE YOU STRONG ENOUGH TO BE VULNERABLE?

The privilege of a lifetime is to become who you truly are.
—JOSEPH CAMPBELL, *A JOSEPH CAMPBELL COMPANION*

IT MAY SEEM COUNTERINTUITIVE TO ASSOCIATE BRAVERY WITH VULnerability, but choosing to be vulnerable is actually the toughest and most courageous decision a man can make. Men being controlled by their fear is the opposite of bravery. They put on a mask of machismo, detachment, or arrogance. But to not be vulnerable is what's behind the mask.

As Brené Brown put it in *Daring Greatly*, "Courage starts with showing up and letting ourselves be seen." The last thing most of us men desire is to be seen, really seen. We become frantic with the possibility, and many of us are fully committed and determined to never allow this to happen. Our self-image is too fragile, our deep need for approval and affirmation from others controls us, and we quiver at the thought of someone uncovering the true, hidden us. And if you hate or reject this hidden version of yourself, your natural assumption is that, if others truly saw you, they would respond in the same way. The bottom line is that conditional love and acceptance are the destroyers of vulnerability and intimacy, and that is as true of your relationship with yourself as it is of your connection to others.

Vulnerability, bravery, and strength are required to be truly open and honest with who you are, especially with another person. Letting them into your true story, allowing them to truly see you, helps them realize they are not alone. For me, my true story is that my wife divorced me because I am gay, and I was fired from the Christian nonprofit I had worked at for twenty-seven years.

Vulnerability is allowing others to see your mistakes, your imperfections, your fears, and the ugly side of you. Every time I do this, it's a choice. I so deeply want to be respected and valued, to be seen as someone to emulate and to be liked. When I reveal that I'm divorced after twenty-one years or that I'm gay, I perceive judgment and a sense of being disqualified, devalued, or disrespected, and unqualified for being listened to. Brad Pitt says, "To be vulnerable is to own your side of the street, to admit I am those mistakes."[1] I love how he articulated that, and I so resonate with it. It's rough, but it's the core of masculine when we own our foibles, to humbly say, "I made that mistake, and I will make it right" and absorb the consequence.

Recently, I was interacting with a group of thirty-two eighteen-year-olds in a fraternity. I asked them to identify a couple of their fears and to say why they were afraid of those things. I had built some trust with them the previous couple of days in my leadership development through choosing to be honest and vulnerable about my pain and some of the stories from my life, and I was curious to see how vulnerable they would be with me and each other. I chose to let them into who John was, to see parts of my story, and to create a space where they didn't feel alone. When we are appropriately vulnerable, it opens the door to trust and connection. Trust and honest connection nourish authentic relationships.

The young men's answers included the fears of failing school and having to go back home from college, of dying, of being rejected and devalued, and of being lonely.

Interestingly, another fear they mentioned and chose to be vulnerable with was disappointing their mothers. They were afraid of being unable to please her or live up to her standards. I believe this is completely unhealthy. It is alarming that a mother could hold so much dominance over a man's life. In many situations, it shows that her love is conditional and that she manipulates him with her love, dispensing affection based on his obedience to her requests, her world view, her determination of what is right or wrong. She can even manipulate him with her victim mentality as a consequence of something his father may have done, using it to make him feel sorry for her so she gets her way.

After asking about their fears, I decided to go a level deeper. I asked them to tell everyone in the room one of their deepest hurts. You never know where guys will go with this type of question. Will they keep the mask on, or will they take it off and be vulnerable and transparent? Well, they took on the risk of walking into this arena and shared deeply vulnerable stories. It was amazing to watch these young men step into their fear arenas to be vulnerable with each other, to take off their masks with each other and be authentic. My takeaway was that they deeply want honest, authentic relationships. They are lonely and desire connection. We all need to belong, and that type of connection requires vulnerability. Again turning to *Daring Greatly*, Brené Brown said, "Because true belonging only happens when we present our authentic, imperfect selves to the world, our sense of belonging can never be greater than our level of self-acceptance."

This event was a rite of passage at this juncture in their life. They had ended high school and were now commencing a new beginning, a new adventure. What they pretended to be in high school—the mask they wore—could now be tweaked or changed. They could choose to throw off parts of that high school boy and create something different, or they could be better at who they truly were. They didn't come in with their reputation; no one knew who they were. This was a significant male ritual crossroad in their lives, which would affect their male maturation.

ARE YOU STRONG ENOUGH TO BE VULNERABLE?

For example, several men have confided that the only reason they did a sport was because of their parents. Once they were in college, they felt the freedom to explore their creative side, not just their athletic side. I have also seen numerous men choose a career based on their dad's decision of what they should do. I've even seen and heard about significant manipulation and control: if they didn't choose their dad's choice of career, he wouldn't pay for their college education.

In another question, I asked if they had a relative or close friend who committed suicide. Interestingly, 33 percent revealed that someone close to them had committed suicide. One young man was sobbing so hard I got up and embraced him in a hug, holding him until the sobbing finally calmed. Another shared that his mother had remarried and that the new husband had abused his mom. She divorced him, after which they learned that the husband had also sexually abused the young man's sisters. The young man was devastated for them. Another shared that, as a freshman, he made the baseball team, and fellow upperclassmen bullied him relentlessly every day, causing such emotional and mental trauma that he cried every night in bed during that season. Several had been wounded in some way by their fathers.

I could go on with story after story of what mystically happened that evening with those men. It was amazing to me that we had all just met only 48 hours earlier, and there we were already at this level of vulnerability. What was astonishing to me was that, when one of them started to cry and fall apart, those around him touched him by placing their hands on him.

It was a beautiful picture of healthy, appropriate, compassionate masculinity.

When four of them individually became completely unglued from the pain they were sharing, I got up and went over and held each young man until he was able to calm himself down. I'm pretty sure that several of them had never shared this hurt with anyone, especially another man. It was a powerful, masculine moment for all of them.

One reason they had joined the fraternity was for lifelong friendships, and this friendship was forming right there, in a very profound way. Seeing me, an older man and possibly a father figure, embrace each of the four until he was able to get his composure gave them a powerful example to emulate later in life. They desperately needed my masculinity at this vulnerable time. Could feminine power have held them? Of course, but it is a different power and has a different dynamic from masculine imprinting.

When I walk away from these incredible experiences, I never know how they will turn out. I'm always overwhelmed with awe. I can't believe I get to be a part of this mystery that only God puts together for them and for me. I get to provide a different definition of masculinity through my example, one that is drastically different from the unhealthy dominant social norms of toxic masculinity.

In that toxic version of masculinity, in this situation, these men would never have acknowledged their pain. They would have never been vulnerable. Other men would verbally and nonverbally condemn, belittle, and shame the boys for their vulnerability. This sort of toxic masculinity comes from the belief that the way to toughen boys up is to not allow emotion, to shame those who show it, and to do anything to stop the expression of pain. In some weird way, it's men condemning younger men, thinking they are helping them become men. I believe it's a form of misandry, a hatred of, contempt for, and prejudice against men or boys. When men shame other men or boys for weeping over painful and devastating events in their lives under the guise of "toughening them up," it's a travesty. Of course, we should all be able to weather the storms of adversity that will be a part of life, to be resilient, self-controlled, and courageous in our fear, but to deny healthy weeping over painful events is outdated and unhealthy. We need to enter the conversation, not sidestep it. It's tougher to weep than not to weep.

Some of the reality of being vulnerable is that people will reject, abandon, slander, and judge you. When this has happened to me, it's my greatest fear of vulnerability coming true. It has made me sad, and it's painful. I feel vomited on and shamed by them and feel unworthy. They liked me better as the poser, as my untrue self.

It takes strength to deal with these realities. I build strength through resilience and perseverance to keep rising, and then I nurture confidence through the conviction that my true self is worthy and that I'm healthier and at peace because of my alignment with my true self. I get stronger and more convinced that I like the real John, the John I let others see. I refuse to revert to the pretender. I've been to this rodeo many times, and I now don't get bucked off as easily. As Brené Brown says in *Daring Greatly*, "Vulnerability is the true birthplace of intimacy and belonging." The poser has no true intimacy.

There is strength in vulnerability, not weakness. There is strength in the honest expression of pain, and the new masculinity includes the freedom to appropriately express this pain, understanding that it is the pathway to healing. Healing does not occur in hiding, suppressing, or self-hatred of one's God-given emotions.

When women or other men condemn a boy or man for crying, he may internalize society's hatred and judgment, leading to self-hatred. The American Psychological Association listed depression, body image issues, poor social function, substance abuse, and stress as side effects of adhering to unhealthy traditional male roles.[2] Vulnerability flies directly into the face of the old masculine values, and it takes courage to confront them. Where are you in respect to this reality? Is fear dominating you and stopping you from entering your arena, stepping onto the wrestling mat? Fortune favors the bold, the brave, the courageous. Once again, only you can call out your brave by the actions you decide to do. What you lack, believe it or not, is inside you. You must choose to wrestle.

Being vulnerable will help you form deeper friendships, and these friendships will be satisfying and rewarding because of the depth of connection. You will embrace the true you, putting the poser to death. Once this happens, you will be able to accept and love yourself with all your flaws. You will experience courage in a completely different dynamic.

ARE YOU STRONG ENOUGH TO BE VULNERABLE?

Choosing not to please others and not to pose as someone you are not means embracing authenticity. Your authenticity will be attractive, and it will bring hope and provide an example for others to emulate. You will grow in your true confidence, giving a death blow to false confidence. You will become more compassionate and show empathy to others, becoming a better human.

Becoming the true you requires the courage, strength, and fierceness to be vulnerable. It may seem counterintuitive to associate bravery with vulnerability, but vulnerability should be the hallmark for being male. It's actually the toughest and most courageous decision a man can make. There is strength in vulnerability, not weakness. There is strength in honest expression of pain, not knowing the answer, feeling overwhelmed. A true man has the freedom to appropriately express this, understanding it is the pathway to success and strength, as well as to healing. Healing does not occur in hiding, suppressing, or self-hating one's God-given emotions. We must call out the brave in us to allow ourselves to be seen and to stay with our bravery when others don't like what they see. Now that's being fierce, confident, and strong!

BRAVEASS REFLECTION

- Immature relationships lack vulnerable connection; there is no intimacy.

- It takes courage to be vulnerable; fear shuts down honest, open connection.
- Vulnerability is sharing your true story, not wearing a mask, to protect yourself.
- With vulnerability comes the possibility of rejection, slander, abandonment, and judgment; that's why the vulnerable are the heroes.

CHAPTER 12

BRAVEASS VIRTUES

The first and greatest victory is to conquer yourself.

—PLATO

BRAVEASS VIRTUES ARE THOSE WE NEED TO EMBRACE, FORGE INTO our lives, honor, and replicate in younger men, as well as sharpen each other with. These are the virtues that purify strength, bravery, confidence, resilience, and depth of character.

This is what makes them braveass. They will break us and reshape us on the anvil. They will never be easy to conquer, but we must conquer them. We must awaken these lost masculine virtues in each one of us and become them, allowing them to define us. They give definition to our masculinity—

"I am a product of the flames which burnt me; the anvil which forged me; and the will that made me grow formidable instead of breaking."

—JEFF MACH, *THERE AND NEVER, EVER BACK AGAIN: DIARY OF A DARK LORD* a frame, a reference, a routine, a map of true-north manhood that unleashes our masculine power. The following braveass virtues will help us be the men we desire to be. As Sir Edmund Percival Hillary, the famous New Zealand mountaineer who was the first to summit Mount Everest, said, "It's not the mountain we conquer but ourselves."

LEARN HOW TO LEAD YOURSELF

"History is full of men who might have conquered the world if only they could have conquered themselves." When I first read this quote in *Why Are We Bad at Picking Good Leaders?* by Jeffrey Cohn and Jay Moran, I immediately thought, *What areas in my life are unconquered, and how is this affecting me personally and in my career?* To conquer means to successfully overcome and take control. To gain mastery or win by overcoming obstacles or opposition. So, John, what do you need to do to conquer yourself? What obstacles or opposition are blocking you from conquering your world?

I have found that all of life involves obstacles and oppositions that we either conquer or that conquer us. We get through one obstacle, and—boom—the next shows up. For me, I go to a place where there is purpose for each obstacle or opposition. It is the way God has chosen. I need to accept it and then move into it, knowing there is a reason. I let go of thinking it is the wrong way and accept it as the right way forward.

This principle of taking responsibility for leading yourself is the most powerful principle of masculine leadership.

Current leadership dialogue seems to focus on the skill set of how to lead others with a sidebar of leading with integrity, but it's silent on the dynamic of personally leading yourself. Not understanding the lack of this integration deeply impacts the masculine influence.

I'm growing in my conviction that I must be committed first and foremost to learning how to lead myself and successfully overcoming whatever hinders me from fully becoming who I am meant to be, forging the best version of me. When we do that, we garner respect for ourselves and gain confidence and respect from others. Leadership always starts first with learning how to lead yourself.

I have found it is a daily decision to lead myself. It is the number one habit I have been developing for years. When I first started going to the gym to lift weights, I had zero muscle. As I made daily choices to hit the gym and gradually learned technique and form, reps and sets, when and why to rest muscles, and the significance of a scheduled plan, I started growing muscle. I developed a habit, a routine. Of course, there were some days I did not want to go to the gym, but I had to take control and conquer my emotions and get my butt in the gym, regardless of how I felt. Usually, after fifteen minutes, I got into my groove, and I was glad I was there. And if I had a training partner—because of both my accountability and their challenge to push me beyond what I thought I could do—it was golden.

Our biggest challenge will not be leading others but leading ourselves, and if you don't know how to lead yourself, then who would want to follow you? Without this skill, you're not worth emulating.

Remember the movie *Karate Kid*? Unbeknownst to Danielsan, his routine of wax on–wax off was teaching him exactly what he needed and what he would build upon before he started karate training. This daily, disciplined routine was what allowed him to win the matches, and it is what will allow you to win your matches. The master, Mr. Miyagi, believed in getting the fundamentals down; they were the key to success. Put another way, Michael Jordan says, "You can practice eight hours a day, but if your technique is wrong, then all you become is very good at shooting the wrong way. Get the fundamentals down and the level of everything you do will rise." Men who demonstrate this braveass virtue change themselves, believe in themselves, and live their best lives.

SACRIFICE

Everyone is naturally selfish. Selfishness is a concern for one's own welfare at the expense of another. We want our own way and often throw an adult tantrum when we don't get what we want or think we deserve. Sacrifice should be a defining quality for us as men. Self-sacrifice will always have a price, a point of pain because it is self-denial. Saying no to yourself and yes to others diminishes selfishness. It's the number one element in being a dad. You say no to yourself and yes to your children—constantly. It is choosing to put ideals, good causes, and the interests of others ahead of your own interests, desires, or wants, influencing a greater good.

> "Great achievement is usually born of great sacrifice, and is never the result of selfishness."
>
> —NAPOLEON HILL

Self-sacrifice builds self-control, which helps us avoid decisions based on our personal feelings and rather push through for the greater good—not giving in to these temporary emotions—to reach a better decision. Men who demonstrate this braveass virtue build self-control and selflessness.

RESILIENCE

Hardships and struggles are the norm for everyone because life is not fair. Yes, pain, suffering, heartache, and brokenness will enter your life. We all get knocked on our ass personally, in our family, in significant relationships, and in our workplace. I guarantee it: if you don't think so, just wait and see.

We must never let these knockdowns keep us down. We must choose to not detach. We must stand back up, get our legs under us, clear our head and emotions, and then get into position to fight again. Staying down demoralizes us, depresses us, makes us cowards, and opens the door to all kinds of addictive behavior. We must enter the wilderness, where we become resilient as we learn and overcome the brokenness and fear and become men of valor. Valor is when you call out your brave in the face of danger and enter the fight. Our scars become our proof of experiential strength. The crucible forges deep strength on its anvil. This deep virtue of persevering through the dark night creates a man with deep, powerful character traits. We arise anew. Men who demonstrate this braveass virtue allow the things that hurt to forge strength and confidence.

SELF-DISCIPLINE

Self-discipline involves training to follow the rules, keep within boundaries, and correct, corral, and control the mind and emotions. Without discipline, we are vulnerable and susceptible to a breach of our personhood. Discipline is the strongest form of self-love. It's doing what you know needs to be done, even if you don't want to do it. Discipline will involve unpleasantness, pain, and grittiness. It mentors us in avoiding concession to our emotions, thoughts, desires, and temptations. It is always a struggle in the mind to take charge of our body and our feelings. We must break unhealthy patterns of quitting or giving up. Only we are responsible to govern our own life, bringing our thoughts under control.

Are you a puppet to your emotions and impulses? You should command your emotions, anxiety, passions, and desires, rather than being dominated by them. Many times, we simply do not know how to control our emotions, and then they control us. When that happens, we regret the resulting behavior. Out-of-control behavior hurts others and hurts us. We are aware that something is drastically wrong, but we don't know how to control our feelings. We suffer anxiety from painful relationships, fear of failure, social rejection, stressful life events, unresolved issues, and trauma. All of these are pain points that affect our feelings and our sense of well-being. We must learn to take charge of these emotions because they cause us to behave in toxic, addictive, and destructive ways. This involves decisions of self-control.

We must learn to take back the power, to exercise control over our impulses, emotions, and desires. It will take self-discipline, restraint, willpower, and levelheadedness to be braveass. As Marco Pierre White says, "Self-control is true power." Men who demonstrate this braveass virtue have a powerful influence in their own lives and the lives of others.

> "In reading the lives of great men, I found that the first victory they won was over themselves . . . self-discipline with all of them came first."
> —HARRY S. TRUMAN

The practice of discipline makes us sharper, better, and steelier. It is taking control. We choose to give in, compromise when life gets rough and tough. Discipline is the pathway to habits, and habits help us establish routines that define who we are.

Without discipline and self-control, we become weak and susceptible to the influence of people, ideas, and things that bring us little worth on our quest to being the best version of ourselves. Men who demonstrate this braveass virtue are able to withstand and resist attack and have the immense capacity to positively impact their own lives as well as the lives of others.

TAKE RESPONSIBILITY FOR YOUR MISTAKES

You must take ownership of the mistakes you make for yourself and all other relationships. We all have missteps. Taking responsibility is honorable. What you refuse to own will follow you, and it will eventually mark you. Blaming, sidestepping, ignoring, keeping silent, denying, letting another take the fall, and being dishonest are the marks of an adolescent boy, not a man. They are dishonorable. No one can trust a liar, a blame shifter. Being responsible and personally accountable means stepping up to the plate and owning your decisions, remarks, and leadership.

Yes, it's a painful decision that can be followed with lots of slander. Many times, hate will be dispensed to you, but it will bring a deep sense of integrity and peace knowing you did what was right, regardless of the consequences. That's being noble—a lost value in our culture of manhood. Men who demonstrate this braveass virtue will be respected and honored.

"Extreme ownership. Leaders must own everything in their world. There is no one else to blame."

—JOCKO WILLINK AND LEIF BABIN, *EXTREME OWNERSHIP: HOW U.S. NAVY SEALS LEAD AND WIN*

> "When you make a mistake, there are only three things you should ever do about it: admit it, learn from it, and don't repeat it."
>
> —PAUL "BEAR" BRYANT,
> *I AIN'T NEVER BEEN NOTHING BUT A WINNER*

LOVE

Self-love involves how you relate to yourself. It is treating yourself with unconditional acceptance, compassion, and honesty in the areas you find easy to love but also in the areas you don't accept about yourself, those part of the imperfect you. It's those things you hate about yourself. Yung Pueblo says in *Lighter: Let Go of the Past, Connect with the Present, and Expand the Future*, "True self-love is multifaceted and includes radical honesty, positive habit building, and unconditional acceptance." There is a correlation between healing and self-love. Remember, self-love is not giving yourself material objects, those things you can purchase and hold. Self-love is not materialism. It's not the ego of putting yourself first in all situations. It's not self-centered behaviors with a disregard to others; that's arrogance and selfishness.

Integrating healthy self-love affects how you love others. Love for yourself and others are two sides of the same coin. Self-love means being able to accept how God has created you. He unconditionally understands your flaws and loves you in spite of them. He says we are worth having a relationship with, regardless. He discards no one. In all our imperfections and mistakes, he is still committed and faithful to loving us. You may see yourself as less and of no good, but God doesn't. God's compassion has room for everyone. As Franciscan Richard Rohr wrote in *Soul Brothers*, "The Lord comes to us disguised as our life."

Choosing to love will require something from you. Laying down your life for the good of another or laying down your power is the picture. Love is always giving, meeting the needs of another, regardless of whether you like them. It's easy to love those who you like and return the love. It's hard to love those you don't like or respect, who are at odds with you or have hurt you. Love is accepting someone regardless. It's giving dignity and value regardless.

All healthy relationships are built on love, trust, and respect, not on rules or holding someone hostage based on authority or position. It's not a contract you sign but a covenant you keep. The opposite of love is to judge, condemn, reject, belittle, devalue, refuse kindness, hate, cancel, and abandon. It's extremely ugly and hateful, and sadly, it has defined being male. Love will never fail us; it brings out kindness, peace, understanding, goodness, gentleness, self-control, and forgiveness. Love should be an identifying quality that we dispense, not arrogance, anger, selfishness, or self-righteousness. To love will be one of the hardest things you will ever do; that's why it is seldom seen. Men who demonstrate this braveass virtue are healthier, revered, and followed.

BUSTING YOUR BUTT

Busting your butt means you get the job done, whatever it demands. You must put in the hard work others refuse to do because of the laziness, greed, narcissism, or entitlement that is rampant in a culture with no redeeming value.

> "I firmly believe that any man's finest hour, the greatest fulfillment of all that he holds dear, is that moment when he has worked his heart out in a good cause and lies exhausted on the field of battle—victorious."
> —VINCE LOMBARDI, "WHAT IT TAKES TO BE NUMBER ONE"

Why be afraid to demand more, to give more? We all have lazy days, days when we don't want to do anything or get involved. Those too are days you must bust your butt because there is nothing redeeming in laziness or entitlement or wanting others to serve you. We need to call out vigilant discipline. Of course, it's going to be difficult and frustrating at times, but when it's done, you have the inner satisfaction of beating the damn thing. It will take pluck, a don't-give-up-or-give-in attitude, self-discipline, and resolve to ascend, crushing it.

Effort and endurance are the guts of busting your butt. It's the drive to bust your butt in your job, marriage, parenting, and relationships, and in building your physical, emotional, mental, and spiritual well-being. And don't forget: you must be diligent to put in the hustle, to lead yourself in forming the best you. This habit of putting in the effort will pay dividends in the long game. Remember what Thomas Edison said: "There is no substitute for hard work." Men who demonstrate this braveass virtue develop drive and fortitude, and they get the job done!

HONESTY

Honesty is the number one virtue people desire in their leader, hands down. To be honest will require humility; the two go hand in hand. I think they are key virtues everyone wants to see in men. Rick Warren put it this way in his book *The Purpose Driven Life*: "Humility is not denying your strengths; rather it is being honest about your weaknesses." You must first be honest with yourself and then with others. Honesty is the number one component in building trust. The wolf pack that runs counter to honesty includes deception, lying, defrauding, half-truths, pretending, and betrayal. Where you find one, you find the others.

When you are honest, you are one, congruent with yourself and your values. We must hold the line on integrity, on honesty and humility, because few do. Our culture is riddled with dishonesty. Many times, we lie to ourselves, and then we believe the lie, and it is destructive. "Pride makes us artificial, and humility makes us real," Thomas Merton said in *No Man Is an Island*.

When we have done something wrong, which happens more than we are willing to admit, we want to shift the heat onto someone else. Our self-image is fragile, and we can't take what others would say or think about our mistake, so we lie or tell a half-truth. That's being dishonest, and people abhor this.

The great college basketball coach John Wooden often told his players, "Talent is God-given. Be humble. Fame is man-given. Be thankful. Conceit is self-given. Be careful." Being honest may be embarrassing, painful, and tough, but the end result will be respect. When you find honesty, look around; you will also find humility. Humility is having the self-awareness of our own flaws, acknowledging that we are not perfect, and embracing the courage to agree. Men who demonstrate this braveass virtue of honesty and humility find freedom and self-respect, and others will give them honor.

APOLOGY

Two of the most powerful words are *I'm sorry*, followed by *please forgive me*. When we apologize, we humble ourselves, admitting we did something wrong that was hurtful. At its core, an apology should restore your relationships.

The opposite is having to be right, which is arrogant. Being right then trumps the value of the relationship. A true apology must involve regret, responsibility, and remedy. You must feel genuine sorrow for what you did, you must take responsibility for your actions, and you must be willing to rectify the situation. Anything less than these three is botched and doesn't represent an authentic apology.

Equally powerful is forgiving yourself. Guilt and shame trap and cage us. They harshly remind us of the mistake and rain down self-hate, which often leads to depression. When you can't forgive yourself, it's like walking around with a 100-pound backpack. Sometimes we believe the lie that we must do some type of penitence before we can take the backpack off. And other times we believe the lie that it will never come off. That's bullshit. Forgive yourself right now, cut the 100-pound backpack full of your mistakes off yourself, and throw it off a mountain. No one deserves to be remembered or labeled by their worst moments—no one. Men who demonstrate this braveass virtue show a commitment to restore what they have done wrong and place a high value on relationship.

BATTLE BUDDIES

We need each other. We were never created to be alone; we were created for relationships. When you have a battle buddy, the other can stand shoulder to shoulder with you, to help and bring strength in the horrific times in life that no one is ever immune from. Nothing great ever happened from being alone. In his book *Tattoos on the Heart: The Power of Boundless Compassion*, Greg Boyle writes, "In Africa they believe a person becomes a person through other people."

When we believe we do not need anyone, we buy into

"I think if I've learned anything about friendship, it's to hang in, stay connected, fight for them, and let them fight for you. Don't walk away, don't be distracted, don't be too busy or tired, don't take them for granted. Friends are part of the glue that holds life and faith together. Powerful stuff."

—JON KATZ

the lie that we are superior. Superiority creates a separation from others and arrogance. You stop being a learner, devaluing the gifts, skills, and design of others. We need others for our personal and professional growth. We need battle buddies who we depend on, who can carry us out after being wounded, who won't leave us, and who are committed to our relationship to the end. Battle buddy friendships bring the thunder to each other! Men who demonstrate this braveass virtue form deep, meaningful, significant male relationships for the journey.

INITIATIVE

> "What is initiative? I'll tell you: it is doing the right thing without being told."
> —ELBERT HUBBARD, *LOVE, LIFE & WORK*

The initiator makes things happen. Most see what needs to be done, but few will meet the challenge and get it done. You must be willing to be the first to start something, to jump in the race. Taking initiative is acting and not waiting or procrastinating. Johann Wolfgang von Goethe said, "Whatever you can do, or dream you can, begin it. Boldness has genius, power, and magic in it. Begin it now." The opposite of taking initiative is being a passive observer.

The fear of failure stops action, so you won't do anything. You stand back, hesitate, avoid taking initiative, and simply refuse to get involved. You must decide to step into the situation and take charge. Do you sit around and wait for opportunity to come to you, or do you look for opportunity and act? Many times, it will reflect working without being told what to do or needing supervision, having the drive to accomplish a task. If you want to change your life, you simply need to do it. Action is required for taking initiative. Men who demonstrate this braveass virtue rise to the challenge and act; they make things happen!

BRAVERY

All of life will demand bravery. Courage will always be a choice to alter yourself, a decision to be bold and kick fear between the legs. Being courageous is staring fear in the eye, extinguishing its stronghold. Mark Twain said, "Courage is resistance to fear, mastery of fear, not absence of fear." We must rise up to difficulties because they are a part of life; there is no way around this truth. There is only one direction—forward and through. Bravery is required to transcend obstacles.

Bravery is in everyone. Trust me, it is there; you just need to call it out. The more you call it out and let it rule, the more you build this muscle, becoming braver and more skilled in using your courage. Courage must be brought to the struggle; it honors the struggle. Bravery is required in every facet of our being—physically, emotionally, spiritually, mentally, and relationally. As Maya Angelou says, "Courage is the most important of all the virtues because without courage, you can't practice any of the other virtues consistently." Men who demonstrate this braveass virtue stop being cowards and become men of valor for themselves and others!

AUTHENTICITY

> "This above all: to thine own self be true,
> And it must follow, as the night the day,
> Thou canst not then be false to any man."
> —WILLIAM SHAKESPEARE, *HAMLET*

We are committed to the masquerade. We love the masks we wear that represent the false persona we project, but it splits us into two different men. Many cower at the thought of taking the mask off, revealing their true self. We wear the mask because it represents what we believe is masculine. We want to be accepted, valued, and affirmed, and we are afraid that our true self won't get us the man card affirmation we desperately want to possess.

Herminia Ibarra states in *Authentic Leadership* that the word *authentic* traditionally referred to any work of art that is an original, not a copy. Authenticity will involve being vulnerable, honest, and transparent. Authenticity can't be faked;

> "Authenticity is everything! You have to wake up every day and look in the mirror, and you want to be proud of the person who's looking back at you. And you can only do that if you're being honest with yourself and being a person of high character. You have an opportunity every single day to write that story of your life."
>
> —AARON RODGERS

you're either real or not. It's being honest with yourself and with others. It's a very scary decision because it places us in an unprotected space. Authenticity comes with being present, fully engaged, and vibrant. It's being true to your personality. When we come to grips with being true to who we are and give the death blow to the impostor, we demonstrate authenticity. We can't be authentic when we are committed to imitating another. Authentic men are open and share their journey, their personal struggles, their failures, their successes, and their triumphs.

Being authentic involves having self-awareness. Self-awareness involves transformative experiences—learning, valuing, and changing from life's rough and difficult throw-down experiences. It is allowing these formative experiences to give meaning to our lives. It's framing these experiences in standing up, rising above these challenges, and sharing this narrative with others.

Men who are true to their values and personality and demonstrate this braveass virtue find their true self, build inner strength, are trusted and respected, and are attractive to others. That's authenticity.

HOPE

We should be offering hope in the face of hopelessness. We should be the light that shines in the darkness, illuminating the way forward. Without hope, discouragement and despair rule. Hope is a powerful truth and is desperately needed in our struggles. Hope inspires us to move out of the gloom and into something better. It redefines and moves us into the impossible. Hope inspires belief that the future can be better than our present or our past. Hope moves us forward.

When we bring hope to the hopeless, we stand strong, point, and then lead the way, even when we too are affected by the despair of darkness. We must bring encouragement in the midst of despair. "Hope will never be silent," Harvey Milk said. Think of a world without hope: the clouds of despair, discouragement, depression, and defeat take over. People give up. They are overwhelmed and shut down. Being braveass involves standing up against the darkness.

> "Let your hopes, not your hurts, shape your future."
> —ROBERT H. SCHULLER

We must bring the perspective that a positive outcome is possible, to anticipate goodness and betterment in one's life. We must bring hope to our loved ones in their despair. We must stand shoulder to shoulder with our friends in their moments of discouragement, speaking hope. We must be the beacon of hope to humanity, saying that this, too, shall pass, we will get through it, and we will come out better than when we went in! Men who demonstrate this braveass virtue enrich and empower the lives of those they love, as well as all of humanity.

> "Habits are formed over time with continuous small decisions."
>
> —JAMES CLEAR, *ATOMIC HABITS*

THE RIGHT HABITS

We all have habits, behaviors we have formed that lead us and have shaped us into who we are at this moment in our narrative. Of course, some are good; we are proud of them because they have formed beauty and strength of character that cause deep satisfaction and self-worth. Other habits that rule us cause us harm. They are destructive to our well-being, as well as to others. Everyone has both occurring in them at the same time. Many times, they are at odds with each other when we need to make decisions.

Habits' strength lies in the consistency of repetition. Habits are our daily rituals. We become the habit. Be assured, your habits define both you and your destiny. You must be honest with yourself in taking the first step to establishing the right habits because when you decide to change a habit, it's a decision to transform your life. It will be uncomfortable, as all transformation is, but you're in it for the long game. You must nurture grit and persistence in the transformation.

> "Stop doing all that shit you know you shouldn't be doing and start doing all the shit you know you should be doing."
> —GARY JOHN BISHOP, *UNFU*K YOURSELF*

At times we need to seek out a life coach to form the habit of self-discipline or self-control, like I did as a wrestler and later in life as a bodybuilder. Do we resonate with a habit because it guides us to who we desire to be? The bottom line is that habits are formed by daily consistency and a set of practices—your deliberate daily routines. You must figure out which habits are unhealthy and which habits matter most to you. Men who demonstrate this braveass virtue become who they were meant to be.

BRAVEASS REFLECTION

- Braveass virtues define you. Take a moment and be thankful for what you have accomplished!
- Identify three braveass virtues you need to develop and devise a plan for this to happen.
- What was it about these three braveass virtues that caught your attention?
- Create a strategy for success using the following outline:
  - Why do you need to develop this braveass virtue?
  - What has caused you defeat and discouragement regarding this braveass virtue?
  - Identify five actions you can take to let this braveass virtue become a part of you.
  - Find an accountability partner to share your strategy for success with and talk it through together each week.

- Listen to your self-talk. Is it positive or negative? Get rid of the self-condemnation in your self-talk.
- Visualize the braveass virtue in your daily life.
- As you fall asleep at night, be thankful for what you are learning and how you are changing, even when it wasn't what you wanted.

CALLING ALL MEN

> "If God gives you something you can do, why in God's name wouldn't you do it?"
> —STEPHEN KING, *ON WRITING: A MEMOIR OF THE CRAFT*

Do you hear the trumpet call? Reveille is blasting to wake you up, calling all men to join the revolution—the revolution to overthrow the current order of what it means to be male in favor of a new system defining and living out true masculinity. I'm calling men to a radical change in how we embrace and live out our maleness. Yes, we will bring some of the traditional maleness with us—the healthy, appropriate parts—and we will integrate them with the truths that have been lost and overshadowed by the dishonest male persona and false social systems that have long been ruled.

You must awaken the true purpose of your masculinity.

With continuous steps forward, the past will become dimmer. These virtues are braveass because they will break us and reshape us on the anvil of manhood. As David Brooks says in *The Road to Character*, "In every life, there are huge crucible moments, altering ordeals, that either make you or break you." This is where character is forged. Your virtues reveal themselves in your decisions and behaviors, ultimately defining you.

I resonate with Jocko Willink and Leif Babin in what they say about leadership in *Extreme Ownership: How U.S. Navy SEALs Lead and Win*: "A good leader must be confident but not cocky; courageous but not foolhardy; competitive but a gracious loser; attentive to details but not obsessed by them; strong but have endurance; a leader and follower; humble not passive; aggressive not overbearing; quiet not silent; calm but not robotic; logical but not devoid of emotions; close with the troops but not so close that one becomes more important than another or more important than the good of the team; not so close that they forget who is in charge; able to execute extreme ownership while exercising decentralized command. A good leader has nothing to prove but everything to prove." I believe this also pertains to our masculinity.

Only you can decide that it is time to grow up, to take responsibility, to expose and leave false masculinity, and to embrace and live out true masculinity. Are you willing? Remember what Epictetus said: "Circumstances don't make the man; they only reveal him to himself." Are you ready to move forward, to choose the road less traveled? True masculinity has the power to influence, heal, and bring hope. True masculinity will bring honor and heroism back. It will uplift, encourage, and empower those we touch. The best thing you can do is heal yourself, lead yourself, take responsibility, and chisel out true masculinity.

The brawl will be with yourself, not with external influences. "The beginning of worthwhile living is thus the confrontation with ourselves," Harry Emerson Fosdick said in *On Being a Real Person*. Our moral code is built with sweat and tears, ups and downs, consistency, courage, and inner integrity. It's our inner struggle. Men who forge these braveass virtues are conquering themselves and will conquer whatever life throws their way.

Join the revolution in living out the braveass virtues we need to forge in our lives. These are the virtues we desire to define us. They are noble and honoring. These virtues target true north for us. They end the chaos of the confusion of masculine qualities. We need to remind ourselves of these virtues weekly and have an accountability partner or group to keep us acting them out.

I implore you to decide to overthrow the old masculine ideal and leave the false and unhealthy status. This battle will win you a freedom you have never experienced. Your self-worth, self-confidence, and self-respect will grow. You will become strong in places you were weak. You will fulfill your purpose and destiny. Your masculine power will be seen by all, and it will influence those in your social circles and in your community. And you will fulfill your purpose and destiny. You will be a blessing and a joy, not a curse and a disappointment.

We all have fork-in-the-road moments that shape us. Taking less-traveled roads will teach you transformational lessons. You will be changed. The apex, seminal moment is when you decide to either call out your brave or submit to your fear. It is the most consequential decision influencing which direction in the fork you take—the choice determines everything. And the choice is yours. Your biggest obstacle is your fear. Remember: it will never be a straight line. It's a curvy road, with lots of ups and downs. Just keep recalibrating, get back on the road, and keep moving forward. That's what success looks like. Success will involve joining the revolution to reclaim your masculine power, calling out your brave, conquering adversity, and living out true masculinity.

NOTES

INTRODUCTION

1. Peggy Orenstein, "The Miseducation of the American Boy," *The Atlantic*, January 2020, https://www.theatlantic.com/magazine/archive/2020/01/the-miseducation-of-the-american-boy/603046/.

CHAPTER 1

1. Lily Rothman, "Why Americans Are More Afraid Than They Used to Be," *TIME*, January 6, 2016, https://time.com/4158007/american-fear-history/.
2. Bisma Anwar, "How to Handle Social Anxiety in College," Talkspace, February 2, 2022, https://www.talkspace.com/blog/social-anxiety-in-college/.
3. BJ Foster, "The 5 Biggest Fears of Men," All Pro Dad, accessed June 6, 2023, https://www.allprodad.com/the-5-biggest-fears-of-men/.

CHAPTER 3

1. Shonna Waters, "Reinventing Yourself: 10 Ways to Realize Your Full Potential," BetterUp (blog), January 5, 2022, https://www.betterup.com/blog/reinventing-yourself.

CHAPTER 4

1. Brené Brown, "Shame vs. Guilt," Brené Brown, January 15, 2013, https://brenebrown.com/articles/2013/01/15/shame-v-guilt/.
2. "Trauma," *Psychology Today*, accessed June 6, 2023, https://www.psychologytoday.com/us/basics/trauma.
3. Trauma-Informed Care Implementation Resource Center, "What Is Trauma?" Trauma-Informed Care Implementation Resource Center, Center for Health Care Strategies, https://www.traumainformedcare.chcs.org/wp-content/uploads/Fact-Sheet-What-is-Trauma.pdf.

CHAPTER 5

1. Jennifer Okafor, "What Are the Benefits of a Positive Attitude and Tips to Keep Positive," TRVST, February 20, 2023, https://www.trvst.world/mind-body/what-are-the-benefits-of-a-positive-attitude/.
2. Mayo Clinic Staff, "Positive Thinking: Stop Negative Self-Talk to Reduce Stress," Mayo Clinic, February 3, 2022, https://www.mayoclinic.org/healthy-lifestyle/stress-management/in-depth/positive-thinking/art-20043950.
3. F. H. Norris and L. B. Sloane, "The Epidemiology of Trauma and PTSD," in *Handbook of PTSD: Science and Practice*, eds. M. J. Friedman, T. M. Keane, and P. A. Resick (New York: Guilford Press, 2007), 78–98.
4. Steven M. Southwick and Dennis S. Charney, *Resilience: The Science of Mastering Life's Greatest Challenges*, 2nd ed. (Cambridge: Cambridge University Press, 2018), 15.
5. Larry Hagner, "7 Reasons Why Men Don't Ask for Help," July 18, 2018, in *The Dad Edge Podcast*, produced by Larry Hagner, MP3 audio, 22:54, https://thedadedge.com/why-men-dont-ask-help/.
6. Daniel S. Lobel, "A Culture Obsessed with Blame," *Psychology Today*, January 17, 2021, https://www.psychologytoday.com/us/blog/my-side-the-couch/202101/culture-obsessed-blame.

7. Todd Henry, "Dealing with a Culture of Blame," *Herding Tigers*, podcast, April 4, 2018, https://www.toddhenry.com/captivate-podcast/dealing-with-a-culture-of-blame/.

CHAPTER 6

1. Gurpreet Singh, "Why Do Men Get Angry?" Welldoing.org, September 17, 2018, https://welldoing.org/article/why-do-men-get-angry.
2. Matt Glowiak, Naveed Saleh, "Men & Anger: Causes, Signs, and Anger Management Tips," Choosing Therapy, October 26, 2021, https://www.choosingtherapy.com/men-anger-issues.
3. Glowiak and Saleh, "Men & Anger," https://www.choosingtherapy.com/men-anger-issues.
4. Singh, "Why Do Men Get Angry?," https://welldoing.org/article/why-do-men-get-angry.
5. Glowiak and Saleh, "Men & Anger," https://www.choosingtherapy.com/men-anger-issues.
6. Ryan Martin in "Men & Anger: Causes, Signs, and Anger Management Tips," Choosing Therapy, October 26, 2021, https://www.choosingtherapy.com/men-anger-issues.

CHAPTER 7

1. The outline of my characters emerged after seeing a presentation by Pastor Mike Vincent, who credits the following website for his inspiration: https://radical.net/article/biblical-manhood-unhealthy-masculinity/.
2. Terry A. Kupers, "Toxic Masculinity as a Barrier to Treatment in Prison," *Journal of Clinical Psychology* 61, no. 6 (February 2005): 714, https://doi.org/10.1002/jclp.20105.
3. Kupers, "Toxic Masculinity as a Barrier to Treatment in Prison," 716.
4. Harris O'Malley, "Finding Strength Through Vulnerability," The Good Men Project, November 24,

2013, https://goodmenproject.com/featured-content/finding-strength-through-vulnerability-hesaid.

5. "APA Guidelines for Psychological Practice with Men and Boys," American Psychological Association, August 2018, https://www.apa.org/about/policy/boys-men-practice-guidelines.pdf.

6. R. M. Eisler and J. R. Skidmore, "Masculine Gender Role Stress: Scale Development and Component Factors in the Appraisal of Stressful Situations," *Behavior Modification* 11, no. 2 (1987): 123–136, https://doi.org/10.1177/01454455870112001.

7. M. K. Saurer and R. M. Eisler, "The Role of Masculine Gender Role Stress in Expressivity and Social Support Network Factors," *Sex Roles: A Journal of Research* 23, no. 5 (1990): 261–271, https://doi.org/10.1007/BF00290047.

CHAPTER 8

1. *Merriam-Webster.com Dictionary*, s.v. "honesty," accessed July 6, 2023, https://www.merriam-webster.com/dictionary/honesty.

2. Agnela Duckworth, *Grit: The Power of Passion and Perseverance* (New York: Scribner, 2016).

3. Duckworth, *Grit*.

4. Frederick Douglass, "The Rights of Women," *The North Star*, July 28, 1848, https://www.census.gov/programs-surveys/sis/resources/historical-documents/north-star.html.

CHAPTER 10

1. "The Crisis of Connection: The Value of Male Friendships," Equinox RTC, April 16, 2021, https://equinoxrtc.com/blog/the-crisis-of-connection-the-value-of-male-friendships/.

2. University of California, Berkeley, "Bromances May Be Good for Men's Health: Moderate Stress Encourages Male Bonding, and Prosocial Behavior Makes Them More Resilient to Stress," *ScienceDaily*, March 3, 2016, https://www.sciencedaily.com/releases/2016/03/160303145918.htm.

3. SAGE, "Young Men Are Getting More Out of 'Bromances' Than

NOTES

Romances," *ScienceDaily*, October 12, 2017, https://www
.sciencedaily.com/releases/2017/10/171012091014.htm.

4. Sean Galla, "Guy Friends: Everything You Need to Know," Men's Group, accessed June 6, 2023, https://mensgroup.com/guy-friends/.

5. Jack Davis, "The Importance of Brotherhood and Deep Male Friendships: The Lone Wolf Dies While the Pack Thrives," Uncivilized Man, accessed June 6, 2023, https://uncivilizedman.net/relationships-sex/the-importance-of-brotherhood-and-deep-male-friendships/.

6. Sonora Jha, "Perspective: All the Lonely Men," *Deseret News*, October 12, 2021, https://www.deseret.com/2021/10/12/22722500/perspective-all-the-lonely-men-loneliness-epidemic-male-friendship-feminism.

CHAPTER 11

1. Michael Paterniti, "Brad Pitt Talks Divorce, Quitting Drinking, and Becoming a Better Man," *GQ*, May 3, 2017, https://www.gq.com/story/brad-pitt-gq-style-cover-story.

2. "APA Guidelines for Psychological Practice with Men and Boys," American Psychological Association, August 2018, https://www.apa.org/about/policy/boys-men-practice-guidelines.pdf.

ABOUT THE AUTHOR

John Robert Hatfield is a leadership psychologist that has been working with men for thirty years. He received his BS from Kansas State University and gained a master's degree from the University of Nebraska–Lincoln in college student development and leadership under the Educational Psychology department. He currently is the interim director of fraternity and sorority life at Kansas State University, works as an independent contractor coaching men, and is sought out by fraternities to manage and change the culture in their chapters. He is the founder and CEO of Brave Man Society, an online community and resource that seeks to challenge men's concept of masculinity and coach them in finding the bravery to lead, transform, and reinvent themselves. An innovative leader and national presenter with extensive experience communicating vision and strategic direction, he creates scalable, sustainable, and effective learning solutions with delivery to diverse national and international audiences across all levels of organizations, affiliations, and associations.

John has lived in Zambia and Uganda and has traveled across Europe, and those transformative experiences were so enriching that he now takes men to Nicaragua every May for a one-week service and multicultural experience, as well as to Brazil to get involved in serving the marginalized. In his free time John enjoys hiking, hitting the gym, adventuring, traveling, and reading.

www.ingramcontent.com/pod-product-compliance
Lightning Source LLC
Chambersburg PA
CBHW030517080526
44586CB00011B/230